Additional Praise for
Zombie Banks

"Yalman Onaran's analysis is dead-on. So is his imagery of the dead banks walking among us, stalking and killing the wobbly post-2008 recovery. *Zombie Banks* clearly and scarily puts together all the pieces that explain a financial world again falling apart. Onaran calls out the culpable, from Wall Street's toady Tim Geithner to Ireland's clueless bankers, and writes so lucidly as to render a complex mess understandable."

—John Helyar, co-author of *Barbarians at the Gate*

"This book does an excellent job of pointing out the administrative and political pressures that are rampant. I like the contrast used to make the point that Iceland avoided the major errors. I've always recommended more capital for the banks as the best way out; so does Onaran. The only way is to announce that we will not bail out any firm at any time; that will change their attitude toward more capital. Higher capital requirement puts the risk decision on management and stockholders, where it belongs."

—Allan Meltzer, author, *A History of the Federal Reserve*, and professor, Carnegie Mellon University

"*Zombie Banks*, like the movie *Zombieland*, is a fun romp—until you realize this is not fiction. Onaran effectively expands Ed Kane's thesis from the Thrift Crisis, when only a few U.S. institutions were 'too big to fail,' and shows how the program of declaring the end of insolvency by merely refusing to recognize its existence has grown popular, worldwide. Of course, Onaran can't yet tell us the end of the story, but we can surmise that the longer the trend continues the worse the fallout will be."

—Joseph Mason, professor, Louisiana State University

ZOMBIE
BANKS

Since 1996, Bloomberg Press has published books for financial professionals, as well as books of general interest in investing, economics, current affairs, and policy affecting investors and business people. Titles are written by well-known practitioners, BLOOMBERG NEWS® reporters and columnists, and other leading authorities and journalists. Bloomberg Press books have been translated into more than 20 languages.

For a list of available titles, please visit our Web site at www.wiley.com/go/bloombergpress.

ZOMBIE BANKS

HOW BROKEN BANKS
AND DEBTOR NATIONS ARE
CRIPPLING THE GLOBAL ECONOMY

YALMAN ONARAN

BLOOMBERG PRESS
An Imprint of
WILEY

Published by John Wiley & Sons, Inc., Hoboken, New Jersey.
Published simultaneously in Canada.

For general information on our other products and services or for technical support, please contact our Customer Care Department within the United States at (800) 762-2974, outside the United States at (317) 572-3993 or fax (317) 572-4002.

Wiley also publishes its books in a variety of electronic formats. Some content that appears in print may not be available in electronic books. For more information about Wiley products, visit our web site at www.wiley.com.

Library of Congress Cataloging-in-Publication Data:
Onaran, Yalman, 1969–
    Zombie banks : how broken banks and debtor nations are crippling the global economy / Yalman Onaran.
        p. cm. — (Bloomberg Press)
    Includes index.
        ISBN 978-1-118-09452-5 (cloth); ISBN 978-1-118-18533-9 (ebk);
        ISBN 978-1-118-18532-2 (ebk); ISBN 978-1-118-18531-5 (ebk)

    1. Debts, External—History—21st century. 2. Banks and banking—History—21st century. 3. Economic history—21st century. I. Title.
    HG3891.5.O53 2011
    332'.042—dc23   2011032158

Printed in the United States of America

10 9 8 7 6 5 4 3 2 1

To Dad, who said he bargained with the Grim Reaper to delay the day until this book's publication, and

To Mom, whose habit of playing the devil's advocate in debates taught me to consider opposing views more easily.

Contents

Foreword

Many books have been written about the financial crisis. They are, perhaps, getting better with age. Perspective improves as time passes. Economic truisms that were obfuscated in the informational fog that surrounded the financial crisis are coming back into focus as the fog clears.

In the years leading up to the crisis, we somehow lost our way. We confused "free markets" with "free-for-all" markets. We transitioned from a society that valued hard work and entrepreneurship to one that worshipped housing speculation and financial arbitrage.

In the fall of 2008, we got our comeuppance, as an economy based on over-leveraged consumers, inflated real estate prices, and artificial derivatives products finally collapsed.

The Great Recession was not the product of an inevitable business cycle. It was caused by the excessive risk taking of a number of large financial institutions. Investors and creditors supported them, notwithstanding their high flying ways, because of the perception that the government would not let them fail. The "smart money" played the system.

And the smart money was right.

Instead of using the crisis as an opportunity to clean out the system, we bailed out most of the inefficient institutions and left the bad assets to rot on their balance sheets. Within a year, those who had been bailed out were paying themselves bonuses while many of the bailers were losing their houses, their jobs, or both.

To be sure, some of the stabilization measures undertaken in the United States were dictated by limitations on the legal tools that were available to close down failing institutions in an orderly way. And notwithstanding the shortcomings of our efforts, we did force our banks to raise significant amounts of new capital and dramatically reduce reliance on short-term funding. As a consequence, U.S. banks are much more stable today than their European counterparts.

But as Yalman Onaran points out in this highly readable book, by bailing out mismanaged institutions, we repeated the mistakes of Japan's "lost decade" and of our own savings-and-loan debacle.

By propping up failing firms, we penalized the well-managed institutions and interfered with the basic functioning of the market.

We cannot rely on our capitalist system to allocate resources for their most productive use unless we let the inefficient or mismanaged fail.

We did not force our financial institutions to shed their bad assets and recognize the losses. And the lingering uncertainty about the true extent of those losses makes previously profligate management more risk averse in an economy where prudent risk taking and lending are most needed, particularly by small businesses.

Unfortunately, governments around the globe continue to nurture and support a bloated financial sector built around an unsustainable model. In the United States, we guarantee their mortgages and subsidize their leverage. So beholden is Washington to the big financial players that it can't even make hedge fund managers pay the same tax rates as the rest of us.

To be sure, a healthy financial sector and recovering housing market are essential to our economic future, and not all financial institutions contributed to the crisis.

But we have to accept the fact that financial services and the housing bubble they fueled became a disproportionate part of our global economy and a disproportionate influence over governments throughout the world. Instead of their traditional role of supporting the credit needs of the real economy, financial services became an end to themselves.

The task at hand is to determine how, in defining our regulatory and fiscal priorities, we can downsize the financial sector over time and reallocate resources to areas that will generate lasting jobs and get us back onto a sustainable economic path.

It is essential that we maintain course on the Basel III agreements to substantially increase both the quality and quantity of capital held by internationally active financial institutions, as well as the agreement to impose an additional capital surcharge on the most systemically important. Stronger capital requirements for financial behemoths are the most direct way to constrain their size and imprudent risk taking. Yet, as this book documents, those hard won agreements are already under political attack.

Ironically, the political debate over how to restart the global economy is devoid of any acknowledgement of the role a bloated financial services industry plays in impeding growth. Until government policymakers come to grips with the basic economic truths reflected in this book, our road to recovery will be a very slow and costly one.

SHEILA BAIR
August 2011

Preface

The global financial crisis started much earlier for me than for most other people. I was a finance journalist covering Bear Stearns and Lehman Brothers for *Bloomberg News*. The problems at Bear Stearns surfaced in June 2007, and the bad news didn't let up for one minute until the Wall Street firm's demise in March 2008. Then, just as at a relay race, Bear Stearns handed off the baton to Lehman Brothers—the day Bear's history ended, attention turned to Lehman as the next to go down. Without skipping a beat, I also turned my attention to the bigger investment bank as its final chapter unfolded in the next six months. Even though, for much of the world, the global financial crisis started in September 2008 with the collapse of Lehman Brothers, for me it had been going on for about 15 months by then, and I was already wiped out from working around the clock. However, because the two firms I was tasked with covering were both dead, I had a unique opportunity as well: When my colleagues reported on the global financial system freezing up, I could stop and look back at what had happened to two financial giants that had each been around for about a century.

As I delved into what had gone wrong at both firms, the biggest discovery I made was that nobody completely knew what was going on inside either bank. Every executive I talked to knew one chunk of the business really well and perhaps had some fleeting sense of a few other related departments, but none, including those at the very top, could connect all the dots. I felt as though I was talking to blind men trying to describe an elephant—each was holding a different part of the animal, so one described it as snakelike, another as a sturdy pillar, somebody else as flapping ears. Nobody saw the whole beast. This realization came back to haunt me as I started looking into the attempts at regulatory overhaul in the United States and globally. I kept discovering that bankers, analysts, investors, regulators, and politicians all held some part of the elephant, but there seemed to be nobody with the full picture. That made rewriting the rules of the game very difficult as it had made running Bear Stearns or Lehman Brothers successfully almost impossible. The financial system had become so complicated that no one had all the answers. The complexity had forced everyone—including journalists like me—to become experts in one small aspect of the system while forgetting the bigger picture.

This book is an attempt to connect the dots that are scattered all over the financial landscape—to bring the full animal to life. There are common threads running through the European and U.S. financial realms, and the unresolved troubles of the banking system affect everyone. Irish readers probably won't be shocked to read the stories about their own country, but will be surprised to see the similarities with the other countries and how they all relate to one another.

While there's a historical element throughout the book in explaining how we got into the situation we are in, it's mostly about what the current predicament is and what should be done so we can get out of it. The book comes out as the European Union wrestles with its troubled periphery and the United States with its crippled housing market. It will help make sense of those issues and uncover the solutions. It would be great if I could guide some of the policymakers toward the right solutions. However, even if I can only get some of the public informed well about them, then I can count on the pressure they'll exert on the politicians to do the right thing.

People with no finance background can pick up this book and read it without difficulty. I tried to emulate the way I explain these same issues to my closest friends during private conversations, and most of them don't have any financial expertise. I tried to avoid technical terms and financial jargon, and explained even the most basic term if I had to use it. Yet there's something for the finance professional in this book too. The trader reading *Zombie Banks* may already know the issues directly relating to his line of business but will benefit from seeing the correlations and similarities, just as the lay reader will.

The first two chapters explain the main concept of zombie banking and put it in historical context, especially how it led to Japan's lost decade of the 1990s. The next four chapters are about Europe's problems—its bankrupt states and broken banks, how they relate to each other. Chapter 3 looks at the debt problems of the European Union (EU) periphery—Greece, Portugal, Ireland, and Spain—and how that is connected to the banks' weaknesses in other countries.

Chapters 4 through 6 analyze the banking systems of Germany, Ireland, and Iceland one by one. You may be surprised to see the strongest and most powerful European country in the same list with the weakest and smallest, but you will be even more shocked to read about the similarities in their banks' problems. Although I have focused on these three countries' banks, that doesn't mean they're the only ones with zombie banks, or in Iceland's case, the only example of how to get rid of them. I would have also liked to delve into the French and Italian banking systems, spend more time on Spain's savings banks, and study Belgium's largest bank, the most highly leveraged lender on the continent; I just ran out of time. Making sure this book remained topical and current meant I couldn't spend many more months expanding my research into more troubled banks in other countries. Germany, Ireland, and Iceland provide the best examples to the phenomenon though.

The following three chapters are about the United States. Chapter 7 looks at the U.S. zombies; Chapter 8 highlights the political fights over how to prevent the next financial crisis; Chapter 9 builds a bridge between housing-market woes and the banks. In the last two chapters, the perspective is global. Chapter 10 zooms in on the dangers of derivatives and too-big-to-fail financial institutions, and Chapter 11 suggests solutions to the problems identified throughout the book. Each of these chapters is sprinkled with entertaining and telling stories of bankers, politicians, bureaucrats, firms, and nations.

To get to those stories and understand the national psyche of these different peoples, I traveled to Ireland, Iceland, and Germany in late 2010 and early 2011. I interviewed dozens of people in those countries, as well as many others in the rest of Europe and the United States. Almost everything in quotation marks comes from those interviews, except for a few cases in which I cite a newspaper column or research paper where the view was expressed. There are also dozens of people I talked to whose names aren't mentioned in the book; they requested anonymity for various reasons, and I respected that, as all journalists do. Many of the behind-the-scenes stories come from those unidentified sources. In the spirit of *Bloomberg News* guidelines on such material, if I couldn't reveal the source, I only used the stories that I heard from at least two different people.

Even though I talked to some 100 people for this book and cite many of their views throughout, when there's no attribution, the views expressed are mine. When I interview people for *Bloomberg News* articles, I like to joke that as a reporter I have no views—I only parrot the views of others I've talked to. There's a sliver of truth to that in the sense that the dozens and hundreds of perspectives I'm consistently exposed to as a reporter form my views. My views about zombie banks are derived from everything I've heard and read in the past 14 years as a financial journalist, covering multiple financial crises in various countries, in addition to the research I did specifically for the book. Although as a reporter I shy away from reflecting my own viewpoint in the articles I write, in this book I did not pull any punches. I hope you enjoy that too.

I would like to thank a few people who helped make this book better. Constantin Gurdgiev, Adriaan van der Knaap, Frederick Cannon and my editor at *Bloomberg News*, Robert Friedman, were kind enough to read the whole manuscript and provide valuable feedback. Evan Burton at John Wiley & Sons was instrumental in making it happen, and Meg Freeborn was a great editor to work with. I'm grateful to the dozens of editors I've worked with at Bloomberg in the past 14 years who've helped me become a better reporter and writer. Our editor-in-chief, Matthew A. Winkler, has inspired me to doggedly pursue the truth every time.

There have been many books about how the crisis unfolded and what caused it. This one is to show that despite their claims to the contrary, politicians worldwide have not tackled the structural problems in the financial system underlying that crisis. When you read this book, I hope you can connect the dots between the street protestors in Greece, strikers in Spain, the $4 gas at the pump, and your unemployed neighbor in Alabama. We haven't fixed our banks, and that will prevent us from moving away from these troubles.

Cast of Characters

Joaquín Almunia
European Union competition commissioner—Caught in a tug of war with German authorities over the future of the *landesbanks*.

Gunnar Andersen
Head of Iceland's banking regulator since April 2009

Árni Páll Árnason
Iceland's economy minister since September 2010

Sheila Bair
Chairman of the U.S. Federal Deposit Insurance Corp. 2006–2011—She fought to restrict the use of taxpayer money for the rescue of failing banks and advocated stronger rules to prevent new zombies.

John Bruton
Ireland's prime minister 1994–1997, EU's ambassador to the United States 2004–2009

Joan Burton
Ireland's social protection minister since March 2011—While she was in opposition prior to that, vocal critic of the previous government's lenience toward the banks as they grew and the handling of their troubles when they fell.

Brian Cowen
Ireland's prime minister 2008–2011—His rescue of the nation's banks led to the collapse of the sovereign credit, forcing him to seek financial assistance from the EU.

Alan Dukes
Chairman of Anglo Irish Bank since June 2010—He was appointed to wind down the worst zombie in Ireland and served as finance minister 1982–1986.

Sean FitzPatrick
Founder of Anglo Irish Bank—Anglo Irish Bank grew 700 times in two decades before blowing up spectacularly in 2009.

Timothy Geithner

U.S. Secretary of the Treasury since January 2009, President of the Federal Reserve Bank of New York 2003–2008—He advocated and played a central role in the rescues of the biggest failing U.S. banks in 2008, and he resisted fundamental changes in regulations that would rein them in.

Thomas M. Hoenig

President of Federal Reserve Bank of Kansas City, 1991–2011—He fought to end the too-big-to-fail (TBTF) conundrum. He was sole dissenter in the monetary policy committee of the Fed against keeping interest rates at zero for so long.

Steffen Kampeter

Germany's deputy finance minister since 2009—He was caught between the country's regional politicians and the EU authorities as they haggled over the future of the *landesbanks*.

Ted Kaufman

U.S. Senator from Delaware 2009–2010, head of Congressional Oversight Panel 2010–2011—He introduced legislation to limit the size of banks so they wouldn't get too big to fail, and he was a vocal critic of the banks' handling of the housing crisis.

Enda Kenny

Ireland's prime minister since March 2011—He wanted the banks' bondholders to share in the losses but was rebuffed by the EU leadership on that request.

Brian Lenihan

Ireland's finance minister May 2008–March 2011—He decided to issue blanket guarantee for the liabilities of the nation's banks, which ended up costing more than €100 billion for the public. He died of cancer in June 2011.

Carl Levin

U.S. Senator from Michigan—He has been fighting for strong bank regulations.

Angela Merkel

Germany's chancellor (prime minister) since 2005—She has been resisting the resolution of her country's zombie banks, thereby endangering the future of the EU.

Jeff Merkley
U.S. senator from Oregon—He has been a defender of tough bank regulations.

David Oddsson
Iceland's prime minister 1991–2004, central bank chief 2005–2009—As prime minister, he allowed the nation's banks exponential growth and oversaw their privatization. As central bank head, he refused to build the currency reserves to save them in case of failure.

Henry Paulson
U.S. Secretary of the Treasury 2006–2008—He played a key role in the rescue of the biggest U.S. banks during the financial crisis.

Robert Rubin
U.S. Secretary of the Treasury 1995–1999, Citigroup executive 1999–2009—As Treasury chief, he was instrumental in the repeal of the 1933 law that separated investment and commercial banking. He joined the bank that benefited most from the dismantling of the rule as soon as he left the governmental administration.

Joseph Stiglitz
Winner of the Nobel Prize in Economics 2001, advisor to U.S. President Bill Clinton 1993–1997, Columbia University professor since 2001—He was a strong critic of the U.S. reaction to the 2008 crisis and the soft gloves used to handle the failing banks.

Paul A. Volcker
Chairman of the U.S. Federal Reserve 1979–1987, advisor to President Barrack Obama 2009–2011—In a semiformal White House role, he struggled to convince the president and his economic lieutenants to push for tougher banking regulations. He was father of the Volcker rule, a section of the U.S. financial reform package that restricts risky trading activities of the banks.

José Luis Rodríguez Zapatero
Spain's prime minister since 2004—He has been struggling to pull his country out of recession while restructuring its failed savings banks, but perhaps a bit too slowly. He said he won't seek re-election in November 2011.

PAST & PRESENT ZOMBIES

U.S.
Bank of America
Citigroup

PAST & PRESENT ZOMBIES

Germany
Landesbanks
  BayernLB
  HSH Nordbank
  Landesbank Baden - Württemberg (LBBW)
  WestLB
Commerzbank
Hypo Real Estate (HRE)

Spain
Cajas

Ireland
Allied Irish Bank
Anglo Irish Bank
Bank of Ireland

Iceland*
Glitnir
Kaupthing
Landsbanki Islands

*Not allowed to live as zombies. Were seized and shut down by government 2008.

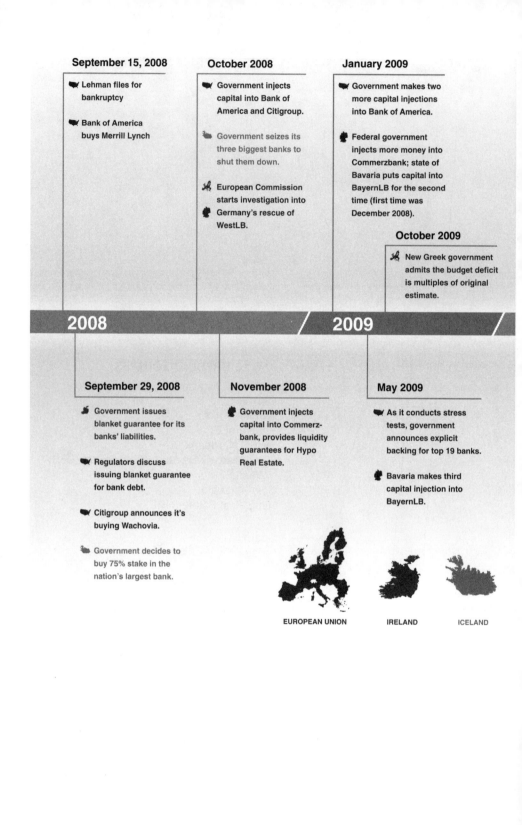

September 15, 2008

- Lehman files for bankruptcy
- Bank of America buys Merrill Lynch

October 2008

- Government injects capital into Bank of America and Citigroup.
- Government seizes its three biggest banks to shut them down.
- European Commission starts investigation into Germany's rescue of WestLB.

January 2009

- Government makes two more capital injections into Bank of America.
- Federal government injects more money into Commerzbank; state of Bavaria puts capital into BayernLB for the second time (first time was December 2008).

October 2009

- New Greek government admits the budget deficit is multiples of original estimate.

2008

2009

September 29, 2008

- Government issues blanket guarantee for its banks' liabilities.
- Regulators discuss issuing blanket guarantee for bank debt.
- Citigroup announces it's buying Wachovia.
- Government decides to buy 75% stake in the nation's largest bank.

November 2008

- Government injects capital into Commerz-bank, provides liquidity guarantees for Hypo Real Estate.

May 2009

- As it conducts stress tests, government announces explicit backing for top 19 banks.
- Bavaria makes third capital injection into BayernLB.

EUROPEAN UNION   IRELAND   ICELAND

July 2010

- Congress passes Dodd-Frank financial reform bill.

March 2011

- Government says remaining zombie banks need 24 billion more capital.

- Spain orders cajas (savings banks) to raise 15 billion capital.

June 2011

- EU struggles to avert Greek default by asking banks to roll over some of their loans to the cash-strapped country.

- The country returns to international capital markets by issuing its first sovereign bond in three years.

2010 / **2011**

May 2010

- EU and IMF announce loan package to rescue Greece.

November 2010

- Government agrees to EU and IMF loan package.

April 2011

- EU-IMF rescue for Portugal.

- Spain's Prime Minister, Zapatero, says he won't run for re-election.

- Courts agree with the government that depositors have priority on claims against the failed banks' assets.

GERMANY

UNITED STATES

Chapter 1

Zombies in Our Midst

T he reason most people today are so scared of zombies could be a fluke of translation. The idea of the flesh-eating zombie depicted in modern-day books and movies originates from a 5,000-year-old epic, in which the goddess of love asks the father of gods to create a drought to punish the man who rejected her love. She then threatens to stir up the dead if her wish isn't granted. Written in Sumerian, Babylonian, and other ancient languages, naturally there are multiple versions of the epic poem and different translations of those variations. While many translations depict zombies eating food "with" or "like" the living, some drop the preposition all together and have the creatures of the underworld eating humans directly. Zombie banks may not eat people or other banks, but their harm to society, the financial system, and the economy is just as scary.

The origins of the term *zombie bank* are much more recent than the *Epic of Gilgamesh*. The expression was first used by Boston College professor Edward J. Kane in an academic paper published in 1987. It referred to the savings and loans institutions in the United States that were insolvent but allowed to stay among the living by their regulators turning a blind eye to their losses.[1] The term gained prominence in the next decade when it was more widely used to denote Japanese banks, whose refusal to face their losses and clean up their balance sheets was blamed for the industrialized nation's so-called Lost Decade. During the financial crisis in 2008, bloggers, columnists, analysts, and even politicians began using it when talking about the weakest banks in the United States and Europe.

In its simplest form, zombie bank refers to an insolvent financial institution whose equity capital has been wiped out so that the value of its obligations is greater than its assets. The level of capital is crucial for banks, more so than for non-financial companies, because in the event of bankruptcy, a bank's assets lose value faster and to a bigger extent. Thus, when a bank's equity declines significantly due to losses, its creditors panic and head for the door (deposits are insured in most Western economies, so depositors don't run away as easily). Capital is the size of the buffer that protects creditors of a bank from losses.

Even though technically, wiped out capital means bankruptcy and rules in many countries require the authorities to seize a lender in such a condition and wind it down, history is full of examples when that was not done. The dead bank is, instead, kept among the living through capital infusions from the government, loans from the central bank, and what is generally referred to as regulatory forbearance—that is, giving the lender leeway on postponing the recognition of losses.[2] The intention is that economic conditions will improve and losses will be reversed; the bank will be able to make profits over time to cover the remaining losses and return to health.

Yet, there are many shades of gray when it comes to identifying insolvent banks. Publicly available balance sheets don't always tell the whole truth. Kane, who was born during the Great Depression, says the outside estimates about a bank's capital position can't be exact, so when those estimates teeter near the point of insolvency, the bank will have a hard time borrowing new money. "You shouldn't think of zombieness as just a one-zero event, that a bank is or isn't, and that you can prove it," Kane says. "When the estimates of the bank's capital fall near the negative area, then people are not going to lend money to them at reasonable rates. Only the taxpayer will do that."

According to R. Christopher Whalen, investment banker and author, a bank doesn't have to be insolvent at all points in time to be called a zombie. Since early 2009, Whalen has been using the term to refer to the weakest U.S. banks. "When a firm fails and is brought back from the dead by the government and kept alive by ongoing support, then that's a zombie," Whalen says. The institution's true return to health can only be tested when all government backing is off and it can stand on its own, he adds. "These zombies don't eat people, they eat money," Whalen wrote in March 2009.[3] So we don't have to worry about which version of the Epic of Gilgamesh to believe; it's the taxpayer money that zombie banks eat and that's where their harm to society is.

Because today's banks are like black boxes, keeping many of their inner workings to themselves, it's impossible to know whether they're zombies for sure. Thomas M. Hoenig, who was a bank examiner at the Federal Reserve Bank of Kansas City before becoming its president, says he could only tell whether some of today's weakest banks are zombies if he could go in and examine them in the same detailed way. But it's not even possible to examine the largest institutions, at least not in the detail Hoenig would like; if the same resources deployed to study the books of a small community bank were used for Citigroup, the third largest U.S. bank, 70,000 examiners would be needed, according to a Kansas City Fed analysis. About 20 inspectors try to do that job now on behalf of the Federal Reserve Bank of New York and another 70 from the Office of the Comptroller of the Currency, the two regulators responsible for monitoring Citigroup.

The Art of Keeping Zombies Alive

When banks face death due to surging losses in a downturn or financial crisis, authorities resort to multiple tools to keep them alive. Capital injections and liquidity provision are the most common. Governments invest in troubled banks when private capital shies away from doing so due to fears of insolvency. Since the 2008 crisis started, governments from the state of Bavaria to Switzerland to the Netherlands have put some $600 billion of capital into their banks.[4] Although some of that has been paid back or replaced with private funds, as was the case with the largest U.S. banks, most of it still remains, and some nations, like Ireland, were pumping new cash into their institutions as this book was being penned. Central bank lending to weak firms is also crucial—at the height of the crisis, the total lending programs of the U.S. Federal Reserve totaled $8.2 trillion, with another $8.9 trillion of funding provided by the Treasury and the Federal Deposit Insurance Corp (FDIC).[5] While a majority of those have been wound down, $7.8 trillion were still outstanding as of October 2010, according to a tally by Nomi Prins, author of *It Takes A Pillage: An Untold Story of Power, Deceit and Untold Trillions*. Prins adds to that another $6.8 trillion of Freddie Mac and Fannie Mae liabilities taken on by the government, arguing that the two mortgage finance giants' rescue was, in effect, an indirect subsidy to the banks (Figure 1.1). If Freddie and Fannie had collapsed, U.S. banks would have been stuck with

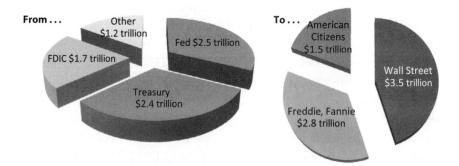

Figure 1.1 U.S. government agencies' spending to prop up the banking system and aid recipients, as of Oct. 2010.
SOURCE: *Bailout Tally Report* by Nomi Prins and Krisztina Ugrin.

massive losses on their $2 trillion holdings of the two mortgage lenders' bonds.[6]

At the end of July 2011, the European Central Bank (ECB) was still providing about $500 billion of short-term funding to the continent's banks. Although the central banks argue such loans are backed by collateral from the banks, data released by the Fed in March 2011 showed that it allowed the use of $118 billion of junk bonds—those with non-investment-grade ratings, meaning higher risk of defaulting— as collateral by the largest banks borrowing from it.[7] The same day that the Fed's crisis lending facts were released, the ECB announced that it would suspend its requirement of accepting only investment-grade bonds as collateral to lend against Irish debt. It had exempted Greek sovereign bonds from its minimum-rating requirement a year earlier, just as rating agencies downgraded the country's debt to below investment grade. That was akin to the ECB saying to Irish banks or others holding Irish government debt, "Don't worry if Ireland's sovereign risk is downgraded to junk; we'll still accept its bonds, just like we accept Greece's junk." The ECB exempted Portugal's government bonds from the rule in July 2011 when they were downgraded to junk ahead of Ireland's debt. Ireland followed suit just a few weeks later.

The money that central banks use to stabilize markets and prevent panic also arrests the decline in asset values, even if that means a property bubble that was at the heart of the crisis to begin with cannot pop all the way. The Fed's purchase of $1.3 trillion of mortgage bonds from January 2009 to March 2010 lowered interest rates on home loans in the United States and stopped the slide of housing prices, even if just temporarily. That slows the zombies' bleeding from losses and lets them write some assets up in value and look solvent.

Another form of assistance to zombie banks is government backing for their debt, old and new. United States banks sold $280 billion of bonds backed by the government before the program was abolished at the end of 2009. European Union banks have used $1.3 trillion of state guarantees.[8] While the explicit guarantees for the banks' debt are being phased out in both continents, implicit guarantees remain. Because the U.S. and European governments have made it clear that they won't let their largest institutions fail, even the weakest lenders are able to borrow private money. The German government's implicit backing for its lenders raises the ratings of its banks by as many as eight levels, credit rating agency Moody's Investors Service says. That means without the so-called support uplift, many would be rated below investment grade. In the United States that uplift is as high as five notches for Bank of America. Without the government backing, the bank's rating by Moody's would drop to just two levels above junk.[9] "The litmus test to be considered truly alive is whether they're able to function without government support of any kind," says Whalen.

Perhaps the biggest subsidy given to all banks in Europe and the United States, though it particularly helps the zombies stay alive, is the near-zero percent interest rate policy maintained by the central banks on both sides of the Atlantic since the start of the crisis. The banks can borrow from their central bank at close to zero and then lend to their own governments at 4 to 10 percent. "That's a backdoor subsidy, and the banks need that subsidy to repair their balance sheets," says David Kotok, chief investment officer at Cumberland Advisors, a long-time critic of the policies. If the banks receive this cash injection long enough, they'll be able to make enough profits to cover their losses from the crisis, some of which are still not recognized.

The delayed recognition of the losses is central to the life zombie banks live. Accounting rules are changed or suspended to let them push out some of their losses to future years; capital regulations are also put on hold to allow for time to rebuild capital; regulators reassure the public and investors that the banks are safe and sound, even when they don't necessarily believe that. The two main agencies responsible for accounting rules in the world—the Financial Accounting Standards Board of the United States and the International Accounting Standards Board—rushed, in late 2008 to early 2009, to tweak regulations that would force banks to recognize declining loan values immediately, as defaults surged. Bank regulators around the world— compelled to tighten capital rules under public pressure—put off the implementation of harsher standards for five to 13 years, knowing that the zombie banks would need all of that time to fix their problems.

Stress tests were conducted by U.S. and EU authorities to show that the largest banks were healthy enough to withstand another crisis. Even though both used optimistic assumptions about the future risks to housing markets and economic shocks, the U.S. test succeeded in assuring investors because it was perceived as full government backing for the top 19 institutions. The EU test failed to gain credibility because it found almost all banks to be healthy when the world knew there was a need for additional capital in many of them. The EU lost further face when the Irish banks, which were given a clean bill of health, collapsed two months after the second stress test in 2010.

Kicking the Can Down the Road

The biggest fear that politicians and regulators have when a bank nears death is the possibility of contagion—that the collapse will spook investors, depositors, and the public in general, causing a run on other banks. So the initial knee-jerk reaction by the authorities is to prevent the fall. Of course, not every failing lender is saved. Small banks around the world get taken over by authorities and wound down all the time; the FDIC in the United States has been seizing one or two every week since the crisis started. This is where the arbitrary judgment on whether a lender is big enough to pose systemic risk comes in. Each government and regulator has its own justification about why a rescue is merited, so there seems to be no easy yardstick for measuring risk. Because these decisions *are* arbitrary and politics plays a significant role, sometimes a smaller bank is rescued while a bigger one is let down. The Federal Reserve subsidized the takeover of Bear Stearns, the fifth largest U.S. investment bank, by JPMorgan Chase in March 2008. Yet six months later, Lehman Brothers, which was twice as big as Bear Stearns, was pushed into bankruptcy because politicians were given the wrong impression that its contagion would be smaller. Spain has refused to seize and shut down its *cajas*, dozens of small savings and loans banks that failed with the collapse of the country's property bubble. Ireland rescued small lenders along with the nation's largest.

There's also a tendency by regulators and politicians to kick the
can down the road because they most likely won't be in positions of
power when things blow up after a few years, says Kane. There's also
the gamble that, if asset prices recover, the economy turns around,
and the zombie bank has enough time to plug its holes with subsidized
profits, then it might actually stand on its own. Some of the savings
and loans that were zombies did turn around and recover from their
ills, Kane notes. And if the gamble on recovery doesn't work, then
hopefully the zombies' collapse will be on the next guy's watch. When
crisis hits and asset values fall precipitously, banks argue that markets
are overreacting, that the values of the mortgages on their books or
the securities they hold are underpriced temporarily due to panicked
sellers. They don't want to be forced to sell at fire-sale prices and
don't want to mark down the remaining assets to what they consider
as unrealistic values. Never mind that the declines are the result of an
asset bubble popping, and that the corrections in values were long
overdue. "When it's a bubble being created, the market is rational,
according to the banks," says Joseph Stiglitz, who won the 2001
Nobel Prize in economics for his work on information asymmetry.
"When the market realizes it was a bubble and starts to correct, then
it's deemed irrational."

Banks' oversized political clout, stemming from their increasing
financial power, helps them convince politicians to rescue them. In
the United States during the past two decades, the banking sector has
outspent all others in campaign contributions and lobbying expenses.[10]
Financial institutions, their employees, and political action committees
have given more money to politicians than the next four top spenders
—health care, defense, transportation, and energy—combined. Bank
executives have the politicians' ears for other reasons too: Henry
Paulson, the U.S. Secretary of the Treasury in 2008 when the latest
crisis started, was running Goldman Sachs, the biggest U.S. investment
bank, just two years earlier. Timothy Geithner, who replaced Paulson
in 2009 as President Barrack Obama's top economic official, was a
protégé of Robert Rubin, who was among the group of executives
running Citigroup when it teetered on the verge of collapse. It should
be no surprise that, during a crisis, those officials turn for advice to
people whom they know well.

Zombies and Lost Decades

It's tempting to think there's a chance that time will heal a zombie's wounds and it will return to the living. However, the problems with letting the zombie banks fester far outweigh the benefits of a possible resurrection.

There are two opposite approaches zombie bank managers take as they struggle to bring their institutions back to life. They'll hoard cash, make few new risky loans, and wait for the slow profit-building to pay for the losses over time. Or they'll take much bigger risks with the hope that they can make windfall profits to plug the holes. The first was employed by Japanese zombie banks in the 1990s and is faulted for that nation's Lost Decade, when the economy couldn't resume growth after the property bubble burst because the banks wouldn't lend. The latter was the choice of action by many savings and loans zombies in the 1980s in the United States as they "gambled for resurrection," in Kane's words. Although some of them won their bets and survived, most saw their losses multiply, making their final resolution even costlier for the taxpayer. We look at both cases and the lessons we refuse to learn from their experiences in the next chapter.

The propping up of institutions that should have died is unfair to healthy competitors. In a real market economy, those companies that take the wrong risks and lose out are supposed to fail, their customers and market share shifting to the surviving firms that were more prudent. In the United States, the credit rating uplift that Citigroup and Bank of America enjoy from their implicit government support lowers their borrowing costs, giving them an unfair advantage over the thousands of small banks that need to rely on their own strength for their ratings. Community banks have to pay more to borrow, because when they mess up and fail, they get taken over and shut down. As the ECB provides short-term loans to Irish banks and other zombies in its region in place of the wholesale borrowing they no longer can access because investors aren't willing to risk their imminent death, banks that fund themselves through more expensive retail deposits lose out. "The business model that was challenged most during the latest crisis, the wholesale funding model, is being rewarded when it should really be punished, curtailed," says Antonio Guglielmi, a bank analyst at Italy's Mediobanca. To compete with the zombies, healthy banks end up taking bigger risks too.

When the zombies offer higher rates to lure depositors, healthier competitors may have to as well so as not to lose customers, thereby hurting their profitability and future health if those rates are unsustainable. The rescuing of failing institutions also creates or increases what's commonly referred to as moral hazard—the propensity of managers to take risk without considering the negative consequences, since they believe the government will bail them out in case the risks blow up in their face one day. If the executives who run their firms to the ground keep their jobs and their companies are resurrected with taxpayer funds each time, then future executives will have very little incentive to worry about the risk-reward balance that is crucial to the functioning of a healthy market economy.

Letting zombies linger around also leaves the financial system vulnerable to aftershocks following a major meltdown. If the recovery takes hold with no hiccups, everything is fine, but too many times, the road isn't so smooth. With zombies around, a second shock will drive down the confidence of investors and customers much faster and bring the financial system to the brink of collapse once again. As much as the public might hate the bankers now, the financial system plays a crucial role in the global economy, allocating capital and moving payments around. A frozen credit market, as we witnessed in 2008, can put the brakes on economic growth.

Keeping interest rates at zero in an effort to give the zombies time to heal their balance sheets has many harmful side effects for the rest of the global economy. It's a wealth transfer from pensioners and others relying on the fixed returns of their savings to the banks' coffers. That transfer reduces the disposable income for a section of society and thus their spending, which can become a major drag on the economy if it lasts for many years. Meanwhile, the rise in government debt is a wealth transfer from future generations, who are forced to pay for their predecessors' mistakes. As in the case of Japan, which has kept its interest rates near zero since 1995, it can also settle in culturally, creating expectations of stable or falling prices and cause delaying of consumption or investment decisions. "Twenty years of zero percent interest rates change the psychology of consumers and savers," says Todd Petzel, chief investment officer at New York fund management firm Offit Capital Advisors. Petzel has calculated that the wealth transfer in the United States equates to $500 billion for each year that rates stay at these levels (Figure 1.2).[11]

Traditionally, lower interest rates are central banks' best weapon to stimulate economic activity. The thinking is that companies will borrow and invest when rates are lower; consumers will borrow and spend. Yet when there are zombie banks in the mix, the money provided at the low interest rate doesn't necessarily trickle down to the consumers or the small enterprises. Zombies that borrow from the central bank at zero would rather lend to borrowers who can afford

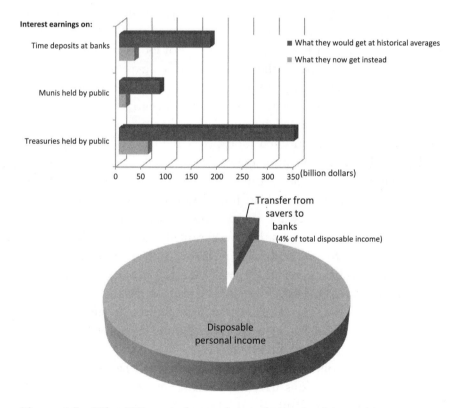

Figure 1.2 What U.S. savers lose each year due to the depressed interest rates, in effect transferring wealth to the coffers of the banks.
SOURCES: Offit Capital Advisors, U.S. Department of Commerce.

to pay higher rates since the zombie needs to heal its broken balance sheet as quickly as possible through profits. Thus, the current zero percent interest-rate policy has channeled funds to emerging market economies where returns are much higher, in double digits in some countries. That has caused overheating of their economies and could cause a crash the way Japan's zero percent policy led to the Asian crisis of 1997–1998 when the free Japanese money found its way to neighboring countries.

Few people have made the connection, but even the events in the Middle East are an indirect result of the monetary easing in the West. Not only have the U.S. and European central banks kept interest rates close to zero, but they've also pumped trillions of dollars of extra cash into the global financial system. This policy of so-called quantitative easing has led to commodity price increases, including agricultural commodities. For the impoverished majorities of Middle Eastern countries, small increases in the cost of food can be devastating and served as a catalyst in the uprisings from Egypt to Tunisia. Last time around, when food prices surged, they came down fast with the financial crisis's onset. This time, the Western central banks are determined to keep pumping money until their banks can earn their way out of death, which can keep food prices high for much longer and lead to further unrest in poor countries.

Bailing out zombie banks can even bring down countries that have been otherwise prudent. Ireland joined Greece in seeking help from the EU in 2010, not because its government spending had been prolific in the past two decades, but because it decided to back its banks that collapsed with the crash of a property bubble. Pumping money into its zombie banks, which have proved to be black holes, almost doubled its national debt and raised fears that it could not sustain paying such a heavy burden. Chapter 5 looks into Ireland's troubles in more detail, and Chapter 6 contrasts Iceland's way of handling its failed banks, by letting them go down.

It's easy for politicians to make mistakes when faced with a crisis considering that decisions have to be made on the fly, with limited information at hand. Paulson and Geithner have said they had to rescue banks otherwise the world could have faced another Great Depression. Perhaps they were right initially—to prevent a total meltdown, temporary measures were needed. However, once the panic subsides, politicians need to seize the opportunity to finish off the business they couldn't during the heat of the moment. That hasn't been done in the three years that have elapsed since the crisis.

Gilgamesh, who was a very good king and loved by his people, made the ultimate error of rejecting goddess Ishtar's love. The ensuing seven-year drought, which Ishtar got the father of gods to inflict through her threat of bringing back the dead, devastated Gilgamesh's empire. Keeping zombie banks alive can wreak similar havoc on the world in the next decade. To prevent a lost decade like Japan's in the 1990s, today's politicians need to kill the zombies so the drought doesn't last longer.

Chapter 2

Lessons Not Learned

Timothy Geithner, who studied Japanese in college and served as the deputy financial attaché at the U.S. embassy in Tokyo in the early 1990s, wrote a memo a few years later to his bosses at the Department of the Treasury, detailing the problems with the Japanese banks. Geithner explained that the country's banks were riddled with losses and couldn't raise capital because investors suspected the value of the assets on their balance sheets to be lower than they'd declared. The memo got to Robert Rubin, then Secretary of the Treasury, who was very impressed with Geithner's analysis and promoted Geithner to Assistant Secretary for International Affairs so he could help with the Asian crisis unfolding after years of zero interest-rate policy in Japan.

Around the same time, Professor Edward Kane penned a paper about the lessons Japan could draw from the mistakes U.S. authorities had made in the handling of their savings-and-loans crisis. Kane presented his paper to the Asian country's finance ministry officials. The Japanese bureaucrats weren't impressed though. They told Kane that his paper was useless because "they were much smarter than the

15

Americans," Kane recalls. Almost two decades later, Geithner seemed to be in the same frame of mind as those Japanese officials. First as the chairman of the Federal Reserve Bank of New York, and again after January 2009 as the Treasury Secretary, Geithner rejected any similarities with Japan and argued that Washington had acted more forcefully and with the right tools. In other words, we're smarter than the Japanese, so why bother with the lessons from their crisis? His inability to see the parallels is hard to fathom when one considers Geithner's own personal experience in Japan and his keen analysis of their problems at the time. Even so, when it comes to the problems of his own country's banks, Geithner seems to have forgotten all the lessons from Japan he once pointed out.

Geithner, other U.S. officials, and their counterparts in Europe have all had the opportunity to learn from past mistakes. Most recently, the U.S. savings-and-loan crisis of the 1980s and Japan's bank crisis in the 1990s give us a blueprint for how not to handle zombie banks. The problems today in the United States and throughout the European Union are like a nasty flashback.

The U.S. Thrift Crisis

Savings and loans banks—also referred to as thrifts or S&Ls—started out with a simple business model in the early nineteenth century. They would pool the savings of the local community to provide home loans to its members. That model worked most of the time in the next two centuries. Even after being devastated by the collapse of the housing market during the Great Depression, the industry made a successful comeback after World War II and accounted for two-thirds of mortgage loans in the country by the 1960s.[1] This simple model exposed the thrifts to a major risk, though: the rise in interest rates. The interest rate they paid out to depositors went up as rates rose, but mortgages were much longer term with fixed rates. This became a real problem in the 1970s and early 1980s when, in an effort to bring down rampant inflation, the Federal Reserve jacked up interest rates consistently all the way up to 20 percent. Inflation was tamed, but many S&Ls had racked up losses as they paid out more than they were taking in.

Instead of shutting down the insolvent thrifts, the regulators over-seeing the industry at the time allowed the weakened institutions to remain in the game with the hope that they would earn their way out of trouble. So the troubled banks doubled down—they expanded outside their traditional area of home mortgages, making loans to and investments in riskier real-estate developments. They also increased their leverage—the amount of money they borrow in relation to their capital—as the regulators lowered capital requirements, so they could make bigger bets. To be able to borrow more, the zombies jacked up the interest rates they were offering depositors, which had to be followed by relatively healthier thrifts as well so they could remain competitive and not lose their depositors. Accounting rules were changed so the S&Ls could book loan-origination fees upfront and postpone the costs of servicing the loan.[2]

When the United States finally came to terms with the problems of the industry and Congress passed a recovery act authorizing their cleanup in 1989, the problems had spread to more institutions and losses had multiplied. In the next six years, authorities closed half of the 3,234 thrifts and transferred their bad assets to a resolution trust to be wound down over time. The house cleaning cost $153 billion, triple the original estimates, most of it borne by the taxpayers.[3]

Japan's Lost Decade

As the United States was coming out of its thrift crisis, Japan was entering its infamous Lost Decade after its property bubble burst. Japan had an asset bubble in the making during the 1980s, when housing prices doubled, stock indices tripled. At the same time, Japanese banks grew to be the world's largest financial institutions, dwarfing their competitors in the United States and Europe. By 1988, nine of the top 10 banks in the world were Japanese, among them well-known names such as Sumitomo, Fuji, and Mitsubishi. Deregulation of the sector led to an increase in riskier lending by the banks as well as loosening of credit standards. The bubble popped at the end of the decade. As house prices started falling and economic growth stagnated, the banks were saddled with bad loans. Their capital base was also shaken because it was largely made up of shares in other companies, and the crash of the stock market reduced the value of those shares.[4]

The banks were hesitant to recognize these losses though. They didn't raise their standard loan-loss reserve ratio—set at 0.3 percent of total lending—even as mortgages and other loans were going bad. Banking regulators, just like their U.S. counterparts dealing with the thrifts' problems a decade earlier, turned a blind eye to this deficiency and allowed them to keep underreporting nonperforming assets.[5] In fact, some critics have claimed that the finance ministry was directing the banks to hide their toxic waste so they would look healthier.[6] The authorities were being lenient toward the weakened banks with the hope that the economy would recover and cure their problems.

The banks had the same hope, so they rolled over bad debt to failing companies with the expectation that they would recover and pay back or at least they would have enough time to make profits over time and recognize the losses then. This evergreening of non-performing loans was widespread during the 1990s in Japan.[7] So the zombie banks created zombie companies, whose death was postponed because banks didn't want to recognize their losses. In 1993, the banks created a bad-debt-resolution firm and transferred some of their non-performing assets there, but this was mostly a ploy to earn tax benefits while still avoiding the real losses. The banks in effect swapped the bad loans on their books with debt from the resolution company, which was also not paying them any interest.[8] Because investors didn't believe in the values of their assets, Japanese banks couldn't raise new capital during this period, but they managed to stay within required capital ratios by selling subordinated debt, which was treated as secondary form of capital. Implementation of new international banking regulations requiring them to increase capital was postponed by regulators.[9]

As the day of reckoning was delayed, it had multiple negative consequences on the Japanese economy. Lending to healthy firms declined while loans to zombie companies were rolled over. Even as the Bank of Japan, the nation's central bank, cut interest rates down to 0.5 percent by 1995, the cheap money didn't filter into the domestic economy (Figure 2.1). Japanese banks instead expanded lending to other Asian countries where they could earn more; they were gambling for resurrection. The banks also preferred to lend to the government since it was more lucrative for them than lending to consumers or corporations and public debt was growing steadily thanks to attempts at fiscal stimulus to jumpstart the economy. In 1996, there

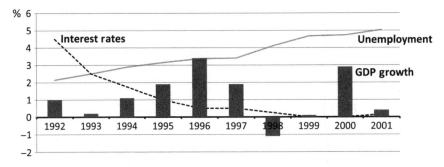

Figure 2.1 Japan's unemployment rate rose steadily as the economy stagnated, even as interest rates were cut to zero.
SOURCES: Bank of Japan, Economic and Social Research Institute (Japan), Bloomberg LP.

was a temporary recovery when the economy grew above 3 percent. The following year, asset bubbles in Thailand, Malaysia, Indonesia, and other Asian countries popped, dumping more losses on Japanese banks who were lending what they borrowed at zero percent from the Bank of Japan to neighboring countries at above 10 percent.[10]

By 1998, the authorities could no longer look the other way because the banks' losses were too large to ignore. In various stages over the next five years, the government and regulators moved to resolve the banking crisis. Initially, they tried to provide capital to the zombie banks. When that didn't work, they nationalized and shut down or merged some of the biggest institutions that were in trouble. They also formed a resolution trust to take over banks' bad assets, and this time they aggressively pushed the banks to comply. When it was all over, the banks had written off about $1 trillion in bad assets, about 20 percent of the nation's annual output. The cleanup cost the government more than $200 billion. Worst of all, Japan's economic growth averaged 1 percent between 1992 and 2002, while unemployment more than doubled to 5 percent.[11]

Even to this day, Japan has not been able to shake off the deflationary trap it was caught in during the crisis. Unemployment has still not come down from the levels it reached during the Lost Decade. The country slips into recession faster than any other developed economy. Following two years of contraction and a temporary recovery in 2010, Japan's economy contracted by 1 percent in the first quarter of 2011, even as most of its peers managed to continue their growth, albeit more slowly. Decades of government's fiscal efforts to stimulate the economy have also boosted Japan's debt level to one of the highest in the world.[12]

Delaying the Fix Increases Costs

Some of the similarities between the current global crisis and Japan's experience two decades ago are easy to spot. The meltdown that started in 2008 was the result of an asset price bubble in the United States and several European countries. Japanese house prices had jumped 142 percent in seven years prior to 1991. The comparable figure was 138 percent for the U.S. housing market until its 2006 peak. In European countries, where the peak occurred in 2007, the seven-year run-up was 136 percent for Spain, 127 percent for the United Kingdom, and 106 percent for Ireland.[13] Banks in Europe and the United States have written off about $1.6 trillion related to the crisis, yet another $550 billion looms, according to the International Monetary Fund (IMF). Interest rates were cut to 0 percent in the United States and 1 percent in the European Union (EU). Although the EU started to increase its benchmark rate in 2011, the U.S. Federal Reserve still has no intentions of doing so three years after having reduced it to zero. The free money from the West is fueling asset-price bubbles in emerging markets, just as it did in Asia in the 1990s.

The United States, and the European Union to a lesser extent, moved to capitalize their troubled banks much faster than Japan did in the 1990s. Still, there are many undercapitalized banks that cannot handle future financial shocks and with too many unresolved bad assets on their balance sheets, the IMF reckons. Damon A. Silvers says an IMF official told him once that there were three stages to every financial crisis: denial, propping up, and nationalization. The longer a country takes to get to the final stage, the more harm is done to its economy, this official told Silvers, who is director of policy at AFL-CIO, one of the largest labor unions in the United States. Silvers says governments moved to the second phase much faster this time around than Japan had done, yet the third and final phase of actually cleaning up the balance sheets of the troubled banks hasn't happened. Anil

Kashyap, a University of Chicago finance professor who has studied the Japanese banking problems extensively, agrees. Even though the troubled banks were forced to raise enough capital to remain technically solvent, they need more capital to expand lending and support economic growth, Kashyap says (Figure 2.2).

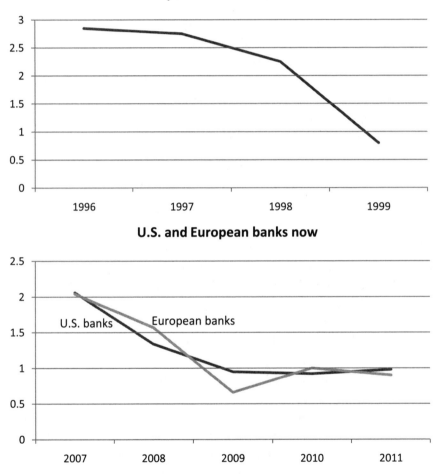

Figure 2.2 The price-to-book value of Japanese banks fell in the 1990s as the troubles on their balance sheets became apparent. The same has happened in Europe and the United States since 2008.

SOURCES: Charles W. Calomiris and Joseph R. Mason, "How to Restructure Failed Banking Systems: Lessons from the U.S. in the 1930s and Japan in the 1990s," in *Governance, Regulation, and Privatization in the Asia-Pacific Region, NBER East Asia Seminar on Economics, Volume 12*, ed. Takatoshi Ito and Anne Krueger (Chicago: University of Chicago Press, 2004), 375–423.

Both the U.S. thrift crisis and Japan's Lost Decade showed that leaving bad assets on the books of banks with weak capital positions results in either reduced lending by those institutions or gambling on resurrection through risky bets. Both crises were solved only after the nonperforming assets were taken off, the losses fully recognized, and the weakest lenders shut down or sold off. That is the most crucial lesson ignored in today's policy response. With accounting rules changed on both sides of the Atlantic so that recognition of losses can be postponed, the U.S. banks are putting off dealing with further losses from the housing market collapse while the EU is delaying the resolution of some member countries' unsustainable debt problems because its banks cannot cope with potential losses. The delay in facing these problems head on is prolonging the housing rut in the United States and the sovereign debt scare in the EU. Even though economic growth recovered in 2010—mostly due to fiscal stimuli and the incredible amount of monetary easing—it can be lost easily when banking problems aren't solved thoroughly, Japan's experience reminds us.

When Japan finally moved to clean up its banking system in the late 1990s, it bought bad assets at deep discounts, which meant some of the weakest banks became insolvent and had to be shut down while others needed further capital injections. Even though the government spent about $495 billion for these efforts initially, it managed to recoup about half its investment when selling the bad assets in the next three years, reducing the final bill for the taxpayer greatly. The resolution of the seized banks and the sales of bad assets didn't disrupt markets.

By providing implicit and explicit guarantees to their major banks, countries from the United States to Ireland have increased the risks for the taxpayers even further during the current crisis, says Professor Kane, who coined the term zombie bank. The strongest lesson he has learned observing the S&L crisis and the Japanese problems is that the final reckoning might be put off for quite some time, despite all the odds, Kane says. When it comes to dealing with today's zombie banks, the same may be true, and it might take another four to five years for the full resolution. As we've seen from the thrift and Japanese crises, that delay will only increase the costs to society and hold back economic recovery.

Chapter 3

Europe's Sovereign Blues

J
ust before Greece adopted the euro in 2001, an analyst at one of the leading European investment banks penned a report concluding that there was something fishy about the country's economic statistics. On the face of it, Greece met most requirements for joining the common currency, but the analyst crunched the numbers over and over, and they just didn't add up. When the report was published, the backlash was amazing: Instead of trying to explain why her math was wrong, Greek officials threatened her personally and demanded that the bank fire their employee. Not being sure how serious the threats were, the analyst's bosses decided to shift her to another division where she would no longer cover anything related to Greece and would have a lower public profile. What is worse is that European Union leaders preparing to admit Greece into the Eurozone weren't interested in hearing the analyst's warnings whatsoever. A bank executive involved in the decision at the time says, "Everybody knew Greece wasn't really ready for the euro. . . . But for political reasons, they wanted Greece in, so they turned a blind eye to its budget gimmicks."

Since then, more cover-ups of Greece's fiscal problems have been discovered, such as the derivatives used to hide some of its obligations, with the assistance of U.S. investment bank Goldman Sachs. Greece's house of cards collapsed soon after a new government that took office in October 2009 came clean with the country's finances, admitting that its budget deficit was multiples of what the outgoing administration had claimed it to be. In May 2010, the European Union (EU) and the International Monetary Fund (IMF) agreed to lend Greece €110 billion to avert the country's default on its debt. A second assistance deal for about the same amount was reached in July 2011 but even that wasn't enough to allay fears of a potential Greek default. The EU's troubles didn't end with Greece either. Ireland and Portugal joined the club in November 2010 and April 2011, respectively, asking for emergency loans from the mother ship. Concern about whether Spain may be the next one to do so goes up and down every few weeks, depending on swings in market sentiment. In July 2011, investors began to be concerned about Italy's debt sustainability as well.

When PIGS Fly

The problems of the European periphery (also referred to as PIGS, using the initials of Portugal, Ireland, Greece, and Spain) aren't all grounded in the same historical reasons. Greece, which wasn't ready to join the currency regime, never righted its ship after becoming a Eurozone member. Its government engaged in profligate spending to provide living standards for its citizens on par with other EU members. Portugal's government finances were stretched in the last decade as the nation was stuck in growth averaging less than 1 percent, even as the rest of the world was living its boom years. Spain and Ireland were hit by the end of a property boom, which saw housing prices triple and quadruple in the past decade. When the bubble burst, their tax revenues collapsed, and employment that had been spiffed up by the construction sector declined massively. Thus, the budget deficits of the PIGS governments jumped in 2009, led by Greece with 15 percent of national output. In 2010, they all came down a bit except that of Ireland, which, in addition to its housing bust, bailed out its failing banks, doubling the deficit. These deficits have bumped up the

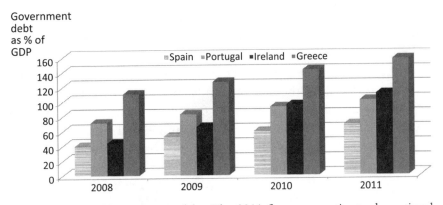

Figure 3.1 PIGS gorging on debt. The 2011 figures are estimates by national or EU authorities as of May 2011.
SOURCES: Eurostat, European Commission, National Treasury Management Agency (Ireland), Banco de España (Spanish Central Bank).

countries' debt ratios, raising concerns about their ability to pay back while their economies contract (Figure 3.1).

The common thread in the PIGS' stories is how they all binged on cheap credit, the way American consumers did during the boom years. The euro, which came into being in 1999 (Portugal, Ireland, and Spain were there at the beginning), brought down borrowing costs for those countries sharply, as the markets' perception of their default risk fell to a level close to that of Germany or France, the powerhouses of the club. Greece was paying more than 20 percent to borrow in the early 1990s, the other three around 10. Euro membership lowered their costs to 3 percent. And so, borrow they did. In Greece, it was the government. In Spain and Ireland, it was households. In Portugal, it was a combination of the two.

This borrowing binge was facilitated by the banks in other Eurozone countries, which were either lending to the PIGS governments, to their banks, or even directly to their consumers as the region's banking system became integrated as envisioned. So as the Germans were saving their hard-earned money, the German banks were funneling that money to consumers, banks, and governments in the European periphery countries, which were spending beyond their means. "Greece, Portugal, Ireland are the subprime of the EU," says Antonio Guglielmi, head of European banking research at Italy's

Mediobanca. "And Spain is the Lehman of Europe." Guglielmi is referring to subprime borrowers in the United States—homeowners with less than pristine credit histories who were offered mortgages nevertheless during that country's housing boom. The U.S. financial crisis was sparked by the collapse of the subprime market. It became a global credit meltdown after the failure of Lehman Brothers, the investment bank that had bet big on subprime and other real estate. Guglielmi thinks Spain's fall will alter the tone of the EU crisis as Lehman's did for the United States.

Zombies in the Pigsty

German, French, and United Kingdom banks led the lending to PIGS and still have the biggest exposure—more than $1 trillion—to the four countries, despite having transferred a big chunk of it to their governments or the European Central Bank (ECB) in late 2010. Another $500 billion of PIGS's external debt is held by other European banks. Most of the remaining $500 billion is on U.S. banks' books (Figure 3.2).[1] German and French voters may be upset that they're bailing out profligate periphery governments, but in fact they're propping up their own banks. Too many German and French banks are too weak to handle the losses that would be caused by the defaults of PIGS or

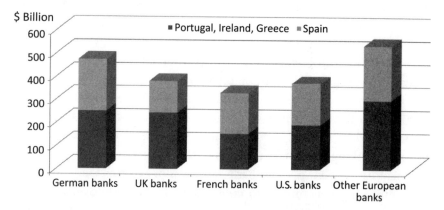

Figure 3.2 Banks' exposures to PIGS. Figures as of the end of fourth quarter 2010, including derivatives and other off-balance-sheet exposures.
Source: Bank for International Settlements.

their banks. As Irish politicians keep pointing out in every meeting, these are not true bailouts: Portugal, Ireland, and Greece haven't been given grants to fix their broken finances. The EU and the IMF are lending them money at 4 percent when the ECB's benchmark interest rate is about 1 percent. In other words, there has been no fiscal transfer from other EU taxpayers to the bankrupt periphery. They've just been given loans to help them pay back the banks. "Emphasis is entirely placed on the mistakes of the borrower, and the lender—the EU banks—is protected financially and intellectually," says John Bruton, who served as Ireland's prime minister from 1994 to 1997. Axel Weber, Germany's central-bank chief until February 2011, confirmed that view in a newspaper editorial when he said financial support for EU members in trouble should only be granted at "nonconcessional rates," and taxpayers in other member states should be protected.[2]

German Chancellor Angela Merkel, who has been calling the shots in the EU during the sovereign debt crisis, is caught in a tough spot. She needs to convince her electorate to support the propping up of Europe's periphery without explaining that it's necessary to prevent the collapse of weak German banks. When public opinion polls show record disdain for banks and bankers since the global financial meltdown in 2008, arguing for bank rescues is much tougher than defending the bailout of other European countries. But the German public is also furious that the Greek government spent beyond its means while letting too many of its civil servants retire at the age of 53, and that the Irish people bought bigger houses than they could afford. So the bailout packages include austerity measures that on the surface are meant to fix the fiscal problems of the receiving countries but are really meant to show the German and French voters that they're being punished for their reckless behavior.[3] Even so, public support is weak for the EU backing of the periphery nations and has been costing Merkel votes in regional elections.[4] Merkel's biggest collaborator is French President Nicolas Sarkozy. The two won't let PIGS or their banks default because they don't want to face the collapse of their zombie banks, European politicians, bankers, and analysts say.

The austerity measures imposed on the periphery nations are a double-edged sword. On one hand, they're trying to correct the fiscal imbalances of the troubled nations. On the other, they're making it harder for the same countries to emerge from recession. Cutting wages of public workers, increasing taxes, and reducing subsidies might help the government save money, but it also eats into the disposable incomes of the citizens and will delay economic recovery further. If the periphery economies cannot grow, their ability to pay back their debt in the long run diminishes even more. So Merkel and Sarkozy are prolonging the inevitable, keeping their zombie banks alive while economies of PIGS stagnate, unemployment surges, and poverty rises. As history shows with Japan or the U.S. thrift crisis, putting off the day of reckoning only adds to the final costs of cleanup.

Putting Lipstick on a Pig

Similar to the treatment of zombie banks in history, the current European zombies are tolerated by regulators through forbearance. A great example of this leniency is the stress tests that EU authorities have been conducting on close to 100 of the largest banks in the union. Although the tests are supposed to measure how the financial institutions would do under losses in a so-called adverse scenario, a possible default by any of the PIGS isn't included in such assumptions. Small haircuts are applied to the banks' portfolios of sovereign debt on their trading book while what's held on the banking book is left intact. Most of the government bonds are held on the banking side of the balance sheet; that's where securities that are held until maturity are recorded, as opposed to the trading side where securities that can be sold any time are logged. Thus, assuming limited losses on the trading book underestimates the real vulnerability of the banks to the sovereign risk. Another weakness of the tests is how banks' capital is calculated. While looking at the capital shortfall of the banks, the EU regulators aren't using the new definitions of capital that were agreed to globally in 2010. The Basel Committee on Banking Supervision, which brings together central banks and regulators from around the world, narrowed the definition of what counts as capital. Yet under intense pressure from Germany and France, the committee delayed the implementation of the new rules until 2018.[5] More important, the tests ignore liquidity risk all together. That's the danger of short-term funding sources running dry when creditors fear the solvency of an institution, as it has happened throughout the current crisis, with Lehman Brothers, Bear Stearns, Ireland's banks, and several German banks.[6]

Banks' exposure to PIGS isn't restricted to holding their government bonds either. German, French and British banks are also exposed to the crashing housing markets and failing banks of the troubled periphery. In Spain, for example, only 16 percent of the German banks' exposures to the country is to the sovereign. The assumptions in the EU stress tests for property price declines aren't realistic. In the adverse scenario, Spain's housing prices are expected to drop about 20 percent from 2011 to 2012, whereas analysts estimate a 30 to 50 percent decline. "European governments want to have it both ways: They want increased confidence in their banking sector, but they don't want to put large amounts of state money into the banks," says Karl Whelan, an economics professor who serves as advisor to the European Parliament's economic affairs committee.

Regardless of the European regulators' efforts to paint their zombie banks as strong enough to deal with all the problems in the region, markets don't trust the zombies and don't lend to them. So they have to rely on the ECB, which is lending about $500 billion to the region's banks. To be able to come up with the collateral required to put up against these loans, some banks are issuing bonds that nobody will buy, according to Constantin Gurdgiev, a finance professor at Trinity College in Dublin. He and many others suspect that the weak German banks also rely on the ECB for funding, though the German central bank doesn't reveal the data. As the ECB lends to zombie banks, it's bailing out their creditors and transferring the risk to taxpayers, who will ultimately have to pay for the postponed losses, says Boston College professor Edward J. Kane.

Spain's Zombies

As markets debate (and change their minds weekly) about whether Spain will be the next member of the periphery nations to request an EU-IMF aid package, its two-term prime minister, José Luis Rodríguez

Zapatero, is struggling to convince the world that his country can survive the crisis without outside help. He has already implemented tough austerity measures to cut the budget deficit, which is suffocating a country already saddled with 21 percent unemployment, the highest in the European Union. After months of street protests, strikes by labor unions and dwindling public support for his harsh economic recipe, Zapatero decided not to run for a third term in the next presidential elections, which he then brought forward by five months to November 2011.[7]

What Zapatero has in his hands—on top of high unemployment, a severe recession and burgeoning debt—is a group of zombie banks whose losses increase as the housing bubble pops. Spain's two biggest banks, Banco Santander and Banco Bilbao Vizcaya Argentaria (mostly known as BBVA), are very international, with more than half their operations in Latin America. They were also well regulated and have high ratios of good capital. However, the Spanish regulators weren't so strict with much smaller *cajas*, their version of the U.S. savings-and-loan banks. The *cajas* loaned heavily to the construction sector during the housing boom, providing half of the €318 billion developers borrowed. The savings banks are stuck with homes and property that are constantly losing value, as well as with mortgages to home-owners and loans to developers that are going sour.[8]

Zapatero injected €15 billion into the troubled banks, which paved the way for a series of mergers in 2010. The Bank of Spain, which regulates the industry, did its version of stress tests and asked the *cajas* to raise €15 billion more capital by September 2011.[9] The government will provide the capital if the banks can't find it on their own by then. Zapatero looks like he's trying to fix the banking problem, but the efforts may be too little, too slow—a typical short-coming of authorities faced with zombie bank issues.

When the Bank of Spain announced the results of its stress tests, markets reacted negatively, finding the capital requirement too low. Analyst estimates of the banks' needs range from €40 billion to €100 billion. The *cajas* refuse the low valuations for their assets that outside investors come up with when discussing possible capital injections. Housing prices, which tripled in the past decade, have only lost 22 percent of their value from the peak and have much more to go. The savings banks are suspected of overvaluing their assets, including houses and land they're stuck with. Moody's rating agency estimates two-thirds of the losses have still not been recognized. Bank-owned properties are expected to triple to 300,000 in 2011.[10] "The *cajas* would be in deep trouble if they reflected the potential 50 percent reduction in housing prices on their balance sheets," says David G. Blanchflower, an economics professor at Dartmouth College.

Like their other zombie brethren, the Spanish zombies are dragging down the healthy banks with them and harming the country's economy as they fight for survival. Because of the uncertainty about their future and concerns about the country's finances, costs of wholesale funding (money borrowed in capital markets) for all Spanish banks have surged. Those have led to increases in interest rates charged to companies, even as the nation struggles to emerge from a severe recession. The savings banks are also offering higher rates for deposits—as zombie banks that are starved for funding and that are gambling for survival do, ignoring the compressed lending margins that might cause. The deposit wars have also hurt the healthy banks' profitability.[11] Spain is repeating the mistakes of Ireland by postponing the resolution of its zombie banks. As Ireland discovered, that delay can end up costing the country much more, and the zombies can bring down the whole nation with them. Just dishing out another €100 billion to the zombies would cause Spain's debt-to-GDP ratio to rise by 10 percentage points. That can increase Spain's vulnerability greatly. But the longer zombies are left to linger, the bigger the losses get, history shows.

When PIGS Stop Flying

The crisis faced by the European periphery isn't unique. Developed and developing countries have been mired in banking and fiscal crises throughout history. To be precise, in their book *This Time Is Different*, Carmen M. Reinhart and Kenneth S. Rogoff count 268 episodes of financial trouble and 199 of external debt defaults since the year 1800.[12] Reinhart and Rogoff also document that there's a strong correlation between those two: Banking crises typically lead to sovereign defaults. Countries usually get out of their rut through restructuring their debt, devaluing their currency, or inflating prices. PIGS cannot devalue or inflate because they're part of a currency union. Other EU member countries don't share the same economic problems, so the ECB is slowly raising interest rates to counter inflation in the wider region while PIGS are stuck in recession and debt overhang. The periphery countries are not allowed to restructure their debt either because that would bring down EU's zombie banks.

"Countries at the periphery are in a huge mess," says Desmond Lachman, a scholar at the American Enterprise Institute for Public Policy Research. "They're being asked to correct imbalances, but they can't restructure their debt or devalue their currency. So when they cut expenditures, their debt loads get heavier because their economies shrink." Lachman thinks the only way out for PIGS is to default on their debt and leave the euro. He's not alone. More and more voices are raised inside and outside Europe to that effect. Even if the periphery countries managed for a while to roll over their debt coming due with the help of EU-IMF loans, their prospects for going back to normal borrowing from markets are looking slimmer. The interest rates demanded by investors—as much 20 percent—are too punishing and not sustainable even for a country in boom times. Even at those rates, many investors have lost their appetites for their bonds, the IMF says.[13]

Meanwhile, as investors turn away from PIGS bonds, the ECB has been buying them, as have the banks in the troubled periphery. Irish banks, which had steered away from Irish government debt during the boom years, have been piling it on since the crisis started. Greek, Spanish, and Portuguese banks are even more exposed to their own government debt—a 50 percent haircut on PIGS sovereign debt would wipe out 70 percent of Greek banks' capital, the Bank of England predicts.[14] So if any of the PIGS default, the ECB, most European banks, and the periphery's own banks would stand to lose money. The ECB has also been financing many of PIGS' banks, so it would also be left with that bill. In other words, the European taxpayer that Germany's Weber and Merkel say shouldn't pay for the problems of the periphery may end up doing so anyway.

The market, while preparing for the defaults and then for periphery nations leaving the Eurozone, may force the inevitable sooner or later. Tyler Cowen, an economics professor at George Mason University, has written about Gresham's law—summed as "bad money drives out good"—at work in the periphery. Depositors in PIGS banks are fleeing because they fear that their money would be converted into less worthy local currency overnight when the country drops out of the euro, Cowen says. That will empty the banks out and make them reliant on state funds to survive, which has already happened in Ireland, he adds. "If two assets—euros inside and outside Ireland—are not equal in value in the eyes of the marketplace, sooner or later the legally fixed price parity will fall apart," Cowen argued in a 2011 editorial.[15] Stuck in such a vicious cycle, the weak EU countries will have no choice but to default and devalue, by abandoning the euro. By refusing to tackle the problem of zombie banks in their midst, Merkel and Sarkozy are steering the EU onto rocky shores and face the danger of losing their most prized asset: the euro. As they drag their feet, the powerful Franco-German duo is also increasing the burden their taxpayers will end up shouldering.

Chapter 4

Germany's Untouchable Zombies

W hen Roman Schmidt was preparing to start his first job after college in the early 1980s, his father was warned by one of his friends about the prospects of the bank that was hiring him. "Why did you allow your son to join a *landesbank*?" the friend asked Schmidt's father at the time. "The *landesbanks* don't have a business model. They'll all merge or be wound down soon." Schmidt didn't stay at WestLB for too long, but the national discussion about the *landesbanks* continued. A few years later, a consultancy firm wrote a report to the German government basically reaching the same conclusion: they don't have a sustainable model any more. The European Commission told the country around the same time that they were hurting competition in the region's financial sector.

Kurt Seitz was working for another *landesbank,* Sachsen LB in the state of Saxony, when a board member came into his office in 2001 to talk about a great idea he had: investing in synthetic assets. Those would be bets on other assets, without ever owning the underlying security—a synthetic collateralized debt obligation (CDO) that would track the performance of some U.S. subprime mortgage bonds, for example. If the bonds did well, the CDOs would pay well. The bonds were all rated AAA, the highest possible. "Nothing ever happens to these papers," Rainer Fuchs told Seitz, but Seitz was suspicious. He had studied debt crises in the United States and didn't like the sound of leveraged wagers on somebody else's bonds. He tried to discourage Fuchs to no avail. Sachsen LB piled on the synthetic stuff and promptly blew up in 2007 when the subprime market came crashing down. Seitz, like Schmidt, had left soon after that conversation, but he watched in sadness as his state's *landesbank* went bust and was merged into a sister institution in 2008.

For some 30 years, Germany has been debating what to do with its troubled *landesbanks*. Many failed and were rescued by the state or federal governments multiple times over the years. Most of them took similar hits, like Sachsen LB during the subprime meltdown, but are still being propped up. They are exposed dangerously to the sovereign bonds of PIGS as well as their real estate markets and banks. Europe's strongest nation, economically and politically, cannot get rid of its *landesbanks,* which almost everyone acknowledges serve no function for the economy any more. The *landesbanks* stand to win the title of the longest-living zombies in global financial history.

Landesbanks in the Land of Banks

Germany's banking system is the most complicated in all of Europe. While Deutsche Bank may be the largest bank and may have the most recognizable name outside of Germany, the country's financial landscape is filled with hundreds of small institutions grouped in several different categories. Even after the 2010 acquisition of a domestic retail bank, Deutsche Bank's share of its home market in most areas is less than 15 percent (Figure 4.1).[1] There are three main groups of lenders in the country, legally recognized as such:

1. Public: This is the biggest pillar of the financial system and is built on 431 savings banks, or *sparkasse.* The *landesbanks,* owned jointly by the savings banks in their region and the states, are also part

Market share by assets

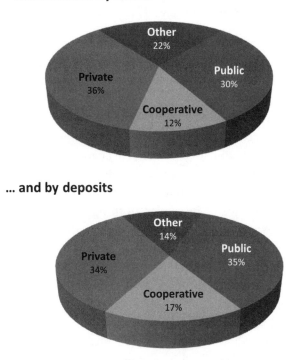

... and by deposits

Figure 4.1 Germany's Crowded Banking Sector: Different groups' shares of the national market as of February 2011.
SOURCE: Deutsche Bundesbank.

of this category. Originally almost each German *land* (state) had one, thus the name *landesbank*—the bank of the state. Through mergers the number has come down to seven.[2]

2. Cooperative: These 1,136 institutions are owned by their 16 million members, who are also depositors. The cooperatives also jointly own two central clearing banks.[3]

3. Private: This group includes the nation's largest banks, such as Deutsche Bank, which are publicly traded. The second largest lender in the country and in this category, Commerzbank, has been partially owned by the federal government since it was rescued during the crisis and is considered in a special category of

a semipublic bank by some.[4] In mid–2011 Commerzbank started paying back the government.

The *landesbanks* were founded at the beginning of the twentieth century. Their original function was to serve as a central clearinghouse for payments, making it possible for the hundreds of small savings banks to transfer money through the system. Over time, they expanded to provide lending and other banking services to larger companies that the savings banks were too small to serve. That involved the opening of branches in other countries since bigger clients, and even many of the small firms exporting their products, needed overseas connections. The *landesbanks* also entered the capital-markets business, originally as clients demanded the service. There was nothing wrong with the original model. The savings banks collected deposits throughout the country and made loans to consumers and small businesses. Yet, there was cash leftover from deposits, so that was channeled through the *landesbanks* to bigger companies, capital markets, and other investments. This way, the savings banks didn't lose expanding local companies as clients to Deutsche Bank or other national institutions. The *landesbanks* were large and diverse enough to provide all the services that such customers needed as they got bigger and opened up to new markets. The two components of the public-bank system complemented each other.

Politics and Banking

The joint ownership by the state governments complicated the equation though. Local politicians had other functions in mind for the *landesbanks*. They wanted the lenders to support economic development in their region, contribute to local charities, and fund pet projects of the local governments. "It's an anomaly that there are state-owned banks in Germany still," says Jan U. Hagen, a finance professor at the European School of Management and Technology in Berlin. "Italian state banks were privatized successfully. France, Spain did the same. Germany is the least developed in this respect." Eike Hallitzky, a member of the Bavarian state parliament and the committee overseeing the region's *landesbank*, BayernLB, gives the following perfect example to this kind of political meddling.

Hallitzky recalls that Leo Kirch, a media mogul who used to own Germany's largest TV station, needed to borrow €2 billion to pay for marketing rights of Formula 1 in 2001. Kirch first went to Deutsche Bank, which refused to lend him any more money since he was seen as pretty much bankrupt at the time and his empire was coming apart. So Kirch went to Edmund Stoiber, the *ministerpräsident* (governor) of Bavaria until 2007, asking for his help. Stoiber asked BayernLB whether it could make the loan to Kirch. The bank's internal credit committee reviewed his finances and rejected the request for the same reasons as Deutsche Bank had. Stoiber didn't give up though. He told his finance minister that the *landesbank* needed to make the loan. The finance minister went to the head of BayernLB and the loan was made. A year later, Kirch's empire totally collapsed, owing billions to German banks, including the €2 billion loan made by BayernLB toward the end.[5] "Why did Stoiber give the money?" asks Hallitzky. "Stoiber and Kirch were old friends. Also, Stoiber was running for chancellor in 2002, so he wanted to have his powerful friends and media backing him. That's how politicians misused the landesbanks."

Because the local politicians saw the *landesbanks* as their cash cows, they also pressed them to make more money so they could provide the funds when needed for these pet projects or political favors. That pushed them to take on bigger risks, such as investing in synthetic CDOs. State ownership also made their financing cheaper—the *landesbanks'* bonds were guaranteed by their respective states, which brought down their borrowing costs. "They started out as clearing centers for the savings banks, but the political aspirations of the stakeholders changed their mission," says Carola Schuler, who covers German banks for Moody's Investors Service, the ratings agency. "They were saying 'why not create regional banks to compete with bigger banks?' Then 'why not international banks?' Especially because they had cheap funding due to government backing."

Cheap Money, One Last Time

In 2001, under European Union (EU) pressure to end the favored status of the *landesbanks*, Germany agreed to phase out the state-backed borrowing and set July 2005 as the end to the practice. What that meant was the state banks had four years to fill up their coffers with guaranteed debt. This was a time when interest rates in Europe and the United States were extremely low, lingering around 1 percent. So the *landesbanks* went on a borrowing binge before the guarantees ran out, raising about €300 billion. Their combined balance sheets swelled to over €2 trillion, reaching the size of Deutsche Bank.[6] Now, on top of the funds the savings banks sent their way, they had much more cash to lend and not enough customers in Germany to do so. They sought opportunities outside the country and found U.S. subprime markets, Icelandic banks, Spanish real estate, and more. They set up off-balance-sheet vehicles to get around capital requirements and off-shore units to escape regulatory scrutiny.

SachsenLB, which was the smallest and newest of the *landesbanks* because it was founded after Germany's reunification, established a subsidiary in Dublin's financial services center, a tax oasis for banks from around the world. Irish banking regulators didn't pay attention to SachsenLB's activities in Dublin and neither did their German counterparts. That allowed the offshore business to invest in U.S. subprime securities almost 80 times its equity capital.[7] "The daughter bank in Dublin was bigger than the mother in Leipzig," says Karl Nolle, a Saxony politician, referring to SachsenLB's headquarters in his state. In 2004, before Nolle's party joined the ruling Christian Democrats in a coalition government to run the state, he wrote numerous letters to his party leaders, warning about the bank's fishy business dealings in Ireland. "I told them 90 percent of profits came from this black box in Dublin; we need to find out what's in it," recalls Nolle. He was told that their new coalition partners didn't want to dig into SachsenLB's doings. "All parties liked the money from the *landesbanks* coming in," Nolle says, adding that the country's central bank and banking regulators were also sleeping at the switch. When SachenLB collapsed, it was sold to Landesbank Baden-Württemberg (LBBW), which took on the losses and risks. Nolle says it was a political favor by the neighboring state's *ministerpräsident* to his counterpart in Saxony, Georg Milbradt, who resigned soon after the bank's sale. LBBW lost €2 billion in 2008 following the merger and another €1.8 billion in the next two years.

Other *landesbanks* also invested in the U.S. subprime market, mostly through complicated instruments such as synthetic CDOs, and they lost even more than SachsenLB. The total subprime losses of the group were $40 billion, and half of that was BayernLB's. The states and the federal government injected $31 billion into them as well as providing some $300 billion of asset and liquidity guarantees.[8]

Even the EU Can't Shut Them Down

Like SachsenLB, WestLB was among the earliest casualties of the subprime crisis because of its bet on the U.S. housing market through complicated securities that blew up first. Although the other *landesbanks* that ran into trouble were rescued by their owners—the state governments and the savings banks—WestLB got a capital injection from the federal government. The EU's competition commissioner started an investigation into the state support for WestLB in 2008.[9] According to EU treaties, member countries cannot prop up their banks in a way that provides unfair advantages to that individual bank over its competitors. Ending the state guarantees for the *landesbanks* in 2005 was the culmination of an earlier investigation by the competition authority, following complaints by the so-called private banks in Germany.

Joaquín Almunia, the EU commissioner, has pretty much ruled that the bank isn't viable under its current format and asked for the sale of the bank or a fundamental restructuring plan. Efforts to sell WestLB have failed after potential buyers were only interested in certain businesses of the lender and not the whole institution. Even after shrinking by about 30 percent, including the transfer of its most toxic assets to a bad bank set up by the federal government, the bank has €192 billion of assets. Almunia has ruled that the authorities overvalued the securities and loans that were shifted to the government's bad bank. Even after getting rid of the bad stuff, WestLB still lost money in 2010.

The bank cannot be sold as a whole because, once out of government ownership, its funding costs would surge and it would lose even more money in coming years. Moody's would lower its credit rating for WestLB from A3, which is still investment grade, to B2, which is five levels below investment grade, when government support is absent. Fitch Ratings would do the same, lowering it to subinvestment level.[10] The assets are also funded by the extra deposits from the region's savings banks, which would also disappear once it's out of the public banking system, says Michael Dawson-Kropf, Fitch's German banking analyst. "It's a business model that only makes sense in state ownership," he says. That hinders even the sale of subsidiaries, which investors have shown an interest in buying. The bank refused to sell its commercial real estate lending unit in 2010, saying the offers were too low.[11] The real story was that potential buyers were asking for state-backed financing for three years after the sale, Moody's analyst Schuler says. The government balked at providing such a guarantee, and the bidders dropped out. The EU had demanded the sale of the unit by the end of 2010. The country had to ask for an extension to the deadline.

Almunia had given Germany until February 2011 to come up with a final plan on what would be done with WestLB as a whole. Three plans were submitted, including one that the bank's management favored and pushed for, basically shrinking the balance sheet further and continuing as before. The commissioner didn't find them specific enough and requested a single blueprint by April. That one foresees a much smaller bank, about one-fourth the size of today's bank, focusing on regional banking and serving the savings banks.[12] That was what the federal government was pushing for earlier, but couldn't get the state of North Rhine-Westphalia—the owner of WestLB—to agree to. Political bickering continued until the last moment, threatening a standoff with the European Commission. The state government failed to get the regional parliament's backing for the revised plan in an initial vote, scrambling to make tweaks to garner support. Steffen Kampeter, Germany's deputy finance minister, who has been holding negotiations with Almunia, complains of the indifference by local officials to EU demands. "For the European Commission, Germany as a nation is relevant. But the owners of the *landesbanks* are the states and the *sparkassen*. So we have a difficult type of discussion—on the one hand with EC and on the other with the state government and *sparkassen*, who don't accept that the EC tells them what to do. They ignore the EC, as they have done for decades."[13]

Almunia is also looking into BayernLB and HSH Nordbank, two other *landesbanks*, though neither the investigation nor the discussions have reached anywhere near those over WestLB. Hallitzky, the Bavarian parliamentarian, says the federal government has had very little influence over the years on the *landesbank* situation. His state's governing politicians aren't trying to resolve the BayernLB problem because they're relying on the EU to do it for them, he suspects. "If the decision is negative, such as have to sell BayernLB, then the state government can point the blame at EU," Hallitzky says.

Irish Connection 2.0

In addition to opening off-shore subsidiaries in Dublin's financial services center, Germany's *landesbanks* also made loans to the country's banking and real estate sectors. At the end of 2010, German banks were owed $29 billion by Irish banks and $86 billion by other non-government borrowers.[14] While specific breakdowns aren't available, analysts suspect the *landesbanks* to be exposed greatly to Ireland's financial and construction industries. The same is true for collapsing property markets in Portugal, Spain, and the United Kingdom. German banks hold about €300 billion of commercial real estate loans—which financed office towers, shopping malls, hotels, or apartment buildings for rent—that are outside the country and those are "in all the hot spots all over the world," according to Moody's analyst Schuler. Most of that is exposure by the *landesbanks*, which invested all the €300 billion they raised before their state guarantees ran out in 2005 into such risky investments. "All that extra cash went to everything high-yielding at the time but turned out not to be high enough to compensate for the risk," Schuler says.

So even if the EU stress tests assumed haircuts on PIGS sovereign debt held by the banks, they wouldn't cover all the risks on *landesbanks'* balance sheets. Because the *landesbanks* can't handle a default by any of the Irish banks, Germany has pressed for their rescue and has opposed any haircuts for the banks' bondholders—that is, the *landesbanks*. The banks' balance sheets are so precarious though that they've been lobbying German regulators to oppose even the slightest bit of tightening in the definition of capital to be used in the stress tests.[15] They were successful in getting German regulators to fight against such tightening during talks on global bank-capital rules. Bundesbank Vice President Franz-Christoph Zeitler, a former Bavarian central bank official, was one of the leading voices representing Germany at the Basel Committee on Banking Supervision. Zeitler, a strong defender of the *landesbanks,* was instrumental in getting other Basel members to agree to the phase-in period of over a decade for banks to replace their lower quality capital with common equity.

Hybrid securities, which count as debt for tax purposes and as equity for regulatory capital calculations, make up about one-third of most *landesbanks'* capital. In WestLB's case, they're 76 percent of the total. These include so-called silent participations, which are unique to German banks. Like preferred securities in the rest of the world, silent participations don't get voting rights, and their dividends can be put off when the firm is losing money. However, just as preferred shares didn't prove to be truly loss absorbing during the latest crisis, the silent participations didn't exactly act like equity capital. Their coupon payments were being made by some *landesbanks* even as the bank was recording losses, according to Fitch. The *landesbanks* were fighting for the recognition by the EU of such hybrid securities as capital in the 2011 stress tests, as they were in 2010. Otherwise, the capital holes in their balance sheets would come to light.

Not all *landesbanks* went on the borrowing binge and made risky investments with their money. A handful stuck to regional lending and has weathered the crisis fairly well. Helaba Landesbank Hessen-Thüringen and Nord/LB, which have avoided big losses, decided to convert their hybrid capital to regular equity in anticipation of the EU stress-test criteria.[16] The ones that managed to stay out of trouble are, in general, majority-owned by the savings banks, which has limited meddling by the states, says Fitch's Dawson-Kropf.

Other German Zombies

The *landesbanks* weren't the only German lenders that blew up during the subprime crisis. Hypo Real Estate (HRE), which was spun off from HypoVereinsbank in 2003, fell apart in 2008 after lending to Icelandic banks and Lehman Brothers and after investing in CDOs and all other types of structured finance. Before its spinoff, HRE was a boring bank—issuing *pfanbriefe,* the German version of covered bonds, and funding commercial real estate projects in Germany. Covered bonds, which are collateralized by the property that the bank lends against, are considered the safest form of funding in European banking because they're conservatively overcollateralized and have never defaulted. The German *pfanbriefe* were the model for the continent's covered-bond market.

But soon after its separation from HypoVereinsbank, HRE shifted its focus to international lending and started borrowing from wholesale markets in addition to its *pfanbriefe*. In 2007, HRE bought DEPFA Bank, which was borrowing short-term to invest in long-duration sovereign bonds. DEPFA had moved to Dublin's financial services center in 2002 to avoid regulation and taxes. HRE kept the unit there after the acquisition to continue taking advantage of both. By 2008, five years after its breakup, HRE had tripled its assets to €420 billion. When short-term funding for structured assets evaporated during the credit crunch, DEPFA collapsed. The bank also lost billions on its structured securities portfolio. The federal government bailed it out with €8 billion of capital injections and provided €124 billion of liquidity guarantees.[17] Deputy Finance Minister Kampeter doesn't want to justify saving HRE. He says the decision was made by the previous boss, Peer Steinbrück, the minister from 2005 to 2009. Others say HRE was rescued because it was a big player in *pfanbriefe,* having issued more than one-fifth of the total, and the government feared the collapse of the whole covered bond market.

The EU competition authorities want HRE to be split in two: public finance and real estate. In three to four years, the real estate unit could be merged with another bank doing the same thing, Kampeter says. Because the European Union hasn't ruled that HRE as an unviable business, the government will let it live, Kampeter says. The bank has shifted €173 billion of toxic assets—including its port-folio of PIGS sovereign bonds—to a bad bank set up by the government.[18] So the risks of the most problematic stuff are now on the shoulders of the taxpayer.

Commerzbank, Germany's second largest, also lost big during the crisis and received the largest capital injection of all German banks. Struggling to be a bigger and better investment bank and to compete with its larger rival, Deutsche Bank, Commerz agreed to buy Dresdner Bank for €10 billion in 2008, just as the credit crisis was starting. Dresdner brought onto Commerz's balance sheet wrong bets on the U.S. subprime market, adding to investments already going sour. The losses forced Commerz to seek government assistance twice. Paying big bucks for Dresdner, just when it needed capital to cover losses, increased Commerzbank's vulnerability. Even insiders admit in private conversations that buying Dresdner brought the bank down. Germany injected €18 billion all together, more than twice the firm's market value at the time.[19]

Just before embarking on Dresdner, Commerz had bought its partners' stake in Eurohypo, a unit specializing in commercial real estate and public finance similar to HRE. Eurohypo has brought losses as well, and it gives Commerz a €17 billion exposure to PIGS sovereign debt. Although EU's Almunia has ordered Commerz to sell Eurohypo, the bank hasn't been successful so far, for similar reasons to WestLB's failure to sell its commercial real estate lending business. It's slowly trying to reduce its sovereign and commercial real estate exposures. The PIGS bond exposure declined by €3 billion during 2010.[20] Commerz's predicaments are similar to the *landesbanks'* because they took similar roads, argues Berlin professor Hagen. "They entered risky businesses in early 2000s in an effort to avoid restructuring that was needed at the time," Hagen says. "They took big risks to com-pensate for the lack of a model."

Even as Commerzbank tries to raise capital to pay back the gov-ernment— it would need to sell triple the amount of shares outstanding right now to cover the whole assistance package—it faces formidable challenges, such as the exposure to periphery countries and rising funding costs. Even though rating agencies bump up its credit score

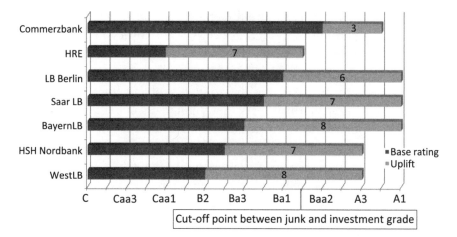

Figure 4.2 How German federal and local governments' backing for banks lift their credit ratings, as of June 2011. The numbers in the uplift boxes show how many levels the government backing boosts a bank's rating; for example, Commerzbank's stand-alone rating of Baa2 is lifted by three levels to A2 due to government support.
SOURCE: Moody's Investors Service.

by three levels, thanks to the government backing (Figure 4.2), the bank's subordinated debt has been downgraded recently after Germany passed a restructuring law that allows regulators to impose haircuts on bonds that are lower on the payment scale. Previously, the seniority of debt would only matter if a bank went bankrupt and was liquidated. Now, junior bonds could face losses even if the bank isn't pushed into bankruptcy. In March 2011, when Commerzbank sold subordinated debt, it had to pay a 2.5 percentage-point premium over its senior bonds, compared to only 0.5 percentage points in the past.[21]

Broken Models, Suffering PIGS

Germany's economy was the fastest growing among the seven richest countries in the last decade, also called G7, according to some measures. Average income grew by close to 1 percent a year, outpacing the United Kingdom, Japan, Canada, United States, France, and Italy between 2001 and 2010. Germany has recovered from the 2008–2009 global recession faster and more forcefully than other rich nations and its European partners.[22] At first glance, these statistics fly in the face of historical precedents of how zombie banks hurt economic growth. But Germany's zombie banks had fueled the spending binges in other EU countries, so not resolving the zombie problem hurts the economies of PIGS, not Germany. As they tighten their belts so they can pay back their debt to German banks, Portugal, Ireland, Greece, and Spain are getting crushed under the weight, and the prospects of their recovery dim. Even Germany started sputtering when its economic growth fell to 0.1 percent in the second quarter of 2011.

German Chancellor Angela Merkel and other German politicians frequently talk about their support for the euro. That's because the common currency has benefited Germany more than other EU countries, says James G. Rickards, who advises fund managers about the intersection of geopolitics and capital markets. The reunification of East and West Germany brought down labor costs in the 1990s, giving the country a competitive advantage when the euro was introduced in 1999, Rickards says. Meanwhile, the declining interest rates in the periphery countries enabled them to buy German exports with borrowed money, fueling the German export machine the country's politicians are so proud of. The *landesbanks*, HRE and other lenders were part of this machine, funneling the extra savings of thrifty Germans. The machine has sputtered, even if the German economy hasn't felt it yet.

Solving the zombie bank problem would shift more of the pain to German taxpayers. Because most of the state-guaranteed debt the *landesbanks* borrowed won't mature until 2015, the debt-holders cannot be forced to share the losses during restructuring. Professor Hagen says the states don't have the money to pay for such a true overhaul—closing them down and merging the central clearing function into one *landesbank* nationwide, which almost everybody agrees to be the solution. The savings banks, which hold equity stakes as well as some of the *landesbanks'* unguaranteed debt, would face losses that could shake the most-trusted pillar of German banking, Hagen suspects. Dr. Thomas Keidel, a director at the association of savings banks, says his members would be willing to cough up funds for such a radical structuring of the *landesbanks*, but regional politics won't allow it to happen. Merger talks between WestLB and BayernLB col-lapsed because Bavaria's governor opposed it, people with knowledge of the discussions say. Regional leaders want to maintain their influ-ence over their cash cows, says Bavarian politician Hallitzky. Another reason they have against such a major overhaul is the potential loss of jobs: 50,000 people work for the *landesbanks*.

What the federal government has done with WestLB and HRE—moving the toxic assets to a bad bank—is the first step of resolving zombie banks. In an economy that's overbanked like Germany, there's no need to keep the remaining good banks alive since their functions can be easily taken up by competitors, though it's proven elusive to close WestLB and HRE so far. Taking on the bad assets of those two banks has swelled Germany's public debt by roughly €300 billion, to 80 percent of national output, the highest level ever. Another €500 billion of toxic sludge from the other *landesbanks* would push the country's debt ratio to over 90 percent. That wouldn't necessarily mean the public debt would increase by as much because there would be some recovery in the bad loans and securities, deputy finance minister Kampeter says. WestLB's bad loans will lose very little if they're sold slowly, according to Kampeter. By 2028, there might be even a gain from some of the assets. "Unlike the Anglo-Saxon model, which wants to solve problems in 24 months, we want to solve them in 24 years," he says.

Kampeter doesn't seem to realize that sitting on the problems usually increases the costs for society, as previous zombie bank epi-sodes have shown. Fitch's Dawson-Kropf is worried that not enough is being done to fix the problems of the banking system before the next crisis hits. "They don't seem to be aware of the time pressure when it comes to fixing the *landesbanks*," he says. Constantin Gurdgiev, a lecturer at Trinity College in Dublin, thinks Germany is kicking the can down the road as much as possible to give its banks time to redeem their outstanding loans to PIGS and thus avoid the losses. For example, by 2013, there would be no Irish bank bonds held by German institutions because they'd be paid back, Gurdgiev says. German banks did cut their PIGS exposure by $96 billion in the fourth quarter of 2010, according to the Bank for International Settlements. Yet the reductions aren't happening because the austerity

packages in Ireland or Greece are helping those countries to pay back
their debt so fast; rather, it's mostly the result of the private debt being
shifted to public debt as the ECB funds the PIGS' banks and the EU
lends to the governments.

So the losses will have to be faced sooner or later, and German
taxpayers will still be on the hook when the ECB's capital has to be
replenished or the EU loans aren't paid back. What's more dangerous
for Germany is the collapse of the euro, which has benefited the
country immensely. Merkel might think she can save her zombie
banks from dying, but she might lose her most precious jewel, the
euro, while doing so.

Chapter 5

Ireland's Zombies Bring the House Down

When delegations from the International Monetary Fund (IMF), the European Central Bank (ECB), and the European Commission arrived in Ireland in November 2010 to negotiate an aid package for the distressed country, the teams settled in the finance ministry building, a baroque structure with Roman columns in downtown Dublin. The staff at the ministry referred to the delegates as Germans, even though they hailed from various countries and only a few were in fact German nationals. But the name stuck because of the general sense among ministry staff that the actual negotiation was being held with Germany, which was calling the shots in the European Union (EU) and dictating the terms at the talks. Germany's political leaders were in the finance ministry building in spirit, even if not physically present, the Irish felt. There were even jokes about whether the ministry staff needed to start learning German. Some of the "Germans" (the IMF delegation) were initially sympathetic to the possibility of the failed Irish banks defaulting on their senior debt, but the real Germans were dead set against it because of their banks' perilous situation and exposure to that debt. The European delegations—from the ECB and the

Commission—said that was not on the table. So the package that
emerged from those talks ended up offering loans for the cash-strapped
country to prop up its zombie banks even more, as well as an agreement that it would use national funds to the same end. Germany's
zombie banks were able to recover their loans to Irish banks while
the Irish government took on more debt to keep its zombies going.

What brought Ireland to its knees in front of the IMF and the
EU was an initial mistake of guaranteeing all the liabilities of its
national banks at the height of the global credit meltdown in 2008.
The government backing was meant to stop the flight of deposits and
restore short-term financing to the Irish banks, and provided some
temporary relief. However, as the underlying problems of the institutions began to emerge in the next two years, and the economy got
worse, exasperating their losses, it looked like the government would
have to make good on its pledge. That was enough to shake investor
confidence in the sovereign credit because the liabilities that were
backed were more than twice the size of the country's gross domestic
product. The banks were rescued all right, but now somebody had
to rescue the country. The government of Prime Minister Brian
Cowen, which was voted out of power in 2011, had two years to do
something about the zombie banks after having secured a temporary
respite from markets with the guarantee. The failure to deal with the
zombies brought down the house of Ireland.

The new government, led by Enda Kenny, has been forced to
follow in the footsteps of its predecessor because it relies on the
IMF-EU funds while its banks survive thanks to ECB financing.
While in opposition, Kenny and the Labour Party had promised the
electorate they would make the German banks share the pain with
the Irish people for the mistakes made during the boom times. Now
the two parties' leaders are resigned to continue implementing the
austerity measures demanded by the IMF, and in July 2011 they
managed to get the EU to lower the interest rate on their emergency
loans as it did for Greece four months earlier. The country struggles
to emerge from a three-year-long recession and continue paying its
debt, which markets doubt it can. "Europe needs to understand the
unemployment impact of all this austerity," says Joan Burton, one of
the most vocal critics of the previous government's fiscal and financial

policies and now a minister from the Labour wing of the coalition. "The important question for the Eurozone is—and this applies to Greece, Portugal, Italy, as well as Ireland: Can you construct a structure to help countries pay their debt? This is the EU's first crisis, they haven't figured it out yet."

The Celtic Tiger's Final Sprint

Ireland earned the nickname Celtic Tiger thanks to an impressive turnaround in its economic prospects following a bleak decade when rising unemployment and poverty led to waves of emigration from the country. In the 1990s, the Irish economy grew at an average annual rate of 7 percent, aided by changes in tax policies as well as EU membership and subsidies. The nation's income per capita, which was two-thirds of the other advanced economies at the beginning of the decade, caught up with them by the end. But once they caught up, the Irish didn't want to slow down. Because the fundamental reasons for the speedy growth had ended, they needed to find something else to spur another decade of it. The European monetary union going into effect around that time and bringing down interest rates for Ireland and the other periphery countries provided them the weapon. The Irish went on a construction and real estate binge, its banks borrowing from German and French banks, its consumers and developers borrowing from the banks (Figure 5.1). The housing boom—with a quadrupling of prices and the share of construction in the workforce doubling—helped maintain the country's annual growth at a 6 percent average until 2008.[1]

The developers and the bankers became the most powerful and revered celebrities. They were aided by tax breaks and other public policies favoring investment in housing and homeownership. The two sectors and their executives had become untouchable, Burton says. Any attempts to curtail the building or the lending frenzy were quashed after heavy lobbying by the banks and the builders. When she or others tried to criticize either industry, they were ignored by supervisory agencies and the government. "There was a conspiracy of silence," Burton says. When economist Morgan Kelly and a few others

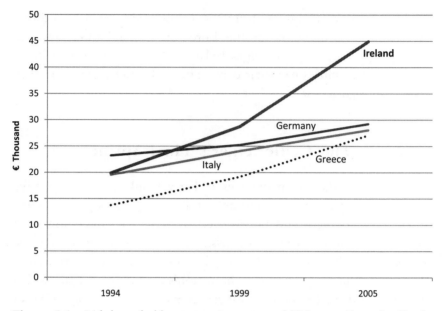

Figure 5.1 Irish household consumption outpaced EU peers. Even the Greeks couldn't keep up with it.
SOURCE: Eurostat.

warned of an approaching housing bust in a series of newspaper articles in late 2006 to early 2007, Bertie Ahern, the prime minister preceding Cowen, derided those "moaning and cribbing about the economy," adding that he was surprised "people who engage in that don't commit suicide." The governing politicians and the regulators often rubbed elbows with the businessmen in both sectors. Of course the taxes paid by the two industries filled up the public coffers—property-related tax revenue had jumped to 17 percent of the total in 2006 from 4 percent a decade earlier. In what became "ghost estates" after the crash, sub-urban residential developments surged, building up small villages near big cities.[2]

Anglo Irish Bank, a relatively newcomer to the financial scene after a merger of two small banks in 1986, led the way in lending to the developers. Sean FitzPatrick's bank grew from €138 million of assets that first year to €97 billion in 2007—basically multiplying its balance sheet 700 times in two decades. Profit surged from €1 million to €1 billion in the same time period, all thanks to the housing boom and its lending to property developers. "Anglo was basically a mono-line," says Alan Dukes, who was appointed chairman of the bank after its collapse. "It had one business line only, and that was lending to property developers." Initially the two big Irish banks, Bank of Ireland and Allied Irish Bank, didn't want to emulate FitzPatrick, but when his profit machine kept churning out stellar results year after year, the other two couldn't help but jump on the bandwagon.

While FitzPatrick opened the way for the lending bonanza to the developers, Anglo Irish didn't lend to homeowners directly. The race to the bottom on that side—residential mortgage lending—was insti-gated by some of the foreign banks that had set up shop in Dublin's financial services center. Bank of Scotland's local unit slashed mortgage rates in 1999, starting a competitive race dubbed "mortgage wars" by the local media. Then, a small lender introduced 100 percent loan-to-value mortgages—the ability to get a home loan without putting any money down, as was popular in the U.S. housing market during its boom—and it spread like a virus, accounting for 36 percent of all mortgages taken out in 2006. By then, the share of property-related lending in the top three banks' balance sheets had risen to 75 percent. Lending to consumers had jumped fivefold as 14 homes were built for every 100 people living in the country. While a handful of econo-mists like Kelly warned of a crash, bankers, politicians, and most analysts talked of a "soft landing" that wouldn't hurt the economy when the housing boom would end.[3] Constantin Gurdgiev, a lecturer at Trinity College and also among the early voices warning about the brewing housing troubles, recalls a dinner party in 2006 when he was seated next to the then-governor of the Central Bank of Ireland. Gurdgiev asked the governor why he wouldn't crack down on 100 percent loan-to-value mortgages. The reply was telling: "The govern-ment will never let me do this."

The first shot across the bow came at the time of Bear Stearns's collapse in March 2008, when the U.S. investment bank was sold at a weekend firesale to JPMorgan Chase. Anglo Irish stock took a beating the Monday after that sale, dropping 15 percent. Although it recovered later during the week, its slide for the rest of the year was consistent, losing about half its value in the next six months. The same happened with the other Irish banks' shares, as investors concerns about their well-being rose when the housing prices started falling and the economy entered a recession. The banks also faced difficulty renewing short-term financing and turned to the ECB for funds while their corporate deposits were fleeing.

The Guarantee from Hell

After Lehman's bankruptcy on September 15, the conditions of the Irish banks deteriorated further, Anglo Irish Bank being in the worst situation. Meetings between government officials and regulators that month involved discussions on whether to nationalize the lender. Pressure on politicians peaked on September 29 when Anglo Irish shares dropped 46 percent as well as sharp declines in all other Irish bank stocks. During meetings late into that night, led by Cowen and his finance minister, Brian Lenihan, the government decided to issue a blanket guarantee on the liabilities of all the banks for two years, including even the subordinated debt, even though their financial advisors from Merrill Lynch had suggested that wasn't necessary. What motivated Cowen and Lenihan was to arrest the flight of deposits and renew confidence in the nation's banking system. Following Lehman's fall, the ECB was telling EU governments that they had to stand behind their banks as confidence eroded, some officials involved in the talks say. Thus, a strong signal had to be given to the markets that Ireland was behind its financial institutions. Nobody in the room was questioning the solvency of the banks, not even Anglo Irish's. They were just looking at the problem as a liquidity crunch. So if financing was restored, the banks would be fine. Some of the meetings that night involved executives of the two biggest banks, Bank of Ireland and Allied Irish, though not Anglo Irish.

Members of the cabinet were roused from their sleep in the middle of the night and asked to sign their names to the decision. Opposition party leaders were told early next morning, some woken by phone calls around dawn. Even though the guarantee was brought to parliament for approval later that week, it was a *fait accompli,* not a real choice given to lawmakers, says Burton, who convinced her colleagues to cast the only dissenting votes, even though they were purely symbolic. Burton confesses that even she wasn't aware of how big the problems with the nation's banks were when she opposed the debt guarantee. She was uncomfortable with the cloud of secrecy behind the decision, the inclusion of subordinated debt, and the lumping of all the banks together, thinking only Anglo Irish was in trouble at the time. "I wasn't aware of the level of destruction that has subsequently emerged in the other two," she says now.

The guarantee provided a two-and-a-half-month respite for the banks only. Despite the guarantee, the banks still weren't able to borrow or raise fresh capital from the markets, deposits continued to rush out, and shares continued falling. They also started admitting losses from their loans to the developers, and the authorities began to realize the problem wasn't only liquidity. In December, the government announced its plans to inject €10 billion capital into the banks. A few days later Anglo chairman FitzPatrick resigned after revelations that he had personally borrowed €87 million from the bank without disclosing it publicly. In January, the government increased the amount it was planning to inject into the top three lenders and effectively nationalized Anglo Irish with the share purchase.[4] But those were just the start. In the next two years, the Irish government had to put in €46 billion of capital into the banks as their losses piled up and their liabilities were backed fully by the state. The banks announced 2009 and 2010 losses that broke records in the nation's corporate history. The bank recapitalizations, coupled with the collapse of property-related tax revenues, caused Ireland's debt to more than double to 96 percent of annual economic output. With no end in sight to either the banks' losses or the economic downturn, investor concerns about Ireland's ability to pay its debt increased, pushing its borrowing costs up. Eventually Cowen's government was forced to request an emergency loan package from the EU and the IMF in November 2010, similar to Greece's six months earlier.[5]

You Can't Burn the Creditors

By the time the IMF delegation rolled into town, the blanket bank-debt guarantee had expired, since it was only for two years, starting in September 2008. Realizing how bad the losses were turning out to be, Finance Minister Lenihan wanted to share the pain with the debt-holders. The IMF folks thought it made sense too. In particular, Anglo Irish, which was being wound down slowly and becoming fully state owned, didn't have to worry about returning to capital markets to borrow in the future, so why not burn its bondholders at this stage, the minister thought. The ECB opposed any losses on senior bonds and was very adamant about that line. "There was very little bargaining in the real sense anyway," said one of the Irish officials who was in the room, recalling the talks a year later. "Take it or leave it, they basically told us. Could we have gone against the wishes of the ECB, which we relied on for funding greatly? No, we couldn't have." Some junior bondholders had incurred losses during voluntary swaps by the banks, but the line on senior debt was very hard. The ECB was concerned about contagion. The central bank was worried that a default on senior debt by the Irish banks could lead to Spanish banks losing their access to funding (and some already have because of troubles with the banking sector there).

Two months after the package was sealed and the bondholders protected once again, Joe Higgins asked European Commission President José Manuel Barroso why saving the lenders to the Irish banks and making the people pay for their reckless lending was sound policy. Barroso, in a heated response to the Socialist deputy representing Ireland in the European Parliament, defended the EU response to the crisis by saying the problems of the Irish banks were completely of their own making and the union was just trying to help a member country.[6] "The reason Barroso got so angry is because there's no moral justification," says Higgins, who's now a member of Ireland's parliament. "There's no moral justification to put on the public's shoulder the billions of euros of bad gambling debts by European banks because of private deals they made with private banks and private developers for private profit." Higgins says he has also been shocked by the secrecy surrounding who the bondholders of the banks are. He called the banks one by one, trying to get lists of their creditors, and was told each time that was confidential information.

Since 2008, Irish banks have been paying off their debt as pieces of it come due, using the government's capital injections as well as increased borrowing from the ECB and the Irish central bank. By March 2011, they relied on €160 billion of short-term financing from the two, which has halved their private debt in the past two years. That, in effect, transfers the future risk of Irish bank losses from their creditors—who were European banks, pension funds, and insurance companies, according to government officials—to the European and the Irish taxpayer. "ECB is becoming the EU's bad bank," says Desmond Lachman, a scholar at the American Enterprise Institute for Public Policy Research in Washington. Even the risk that has been shifted to the Irish government could end up being EU's problem, because Ireland is now borrowing from the union and the IMF since it's been shut out of capital markets, according to Kevin O'Rourke, an economics professor at Dublin's Trinity College and one of the few who predicted the crash early on. "We're removing the bomb from one pocket and putting it in the other pocket," says John Bruton, a former Irish prime minister. "It's not Ireland versus Europe. There's a resistance in Europe to look at the problem as a whole. Otherwise they'd realize that it's actually Europe versus itself."

Not So Innocent EU

When he raised his morality question to Barroso, Higgins says he wasn't accusing the EU of having caused the Irish crisis. "Not that there isn't plenty to blame the EU for—such as the deregulation of the banks they've been pushing for," Higgins adds. Trinity Professor O'Rourke says the failure to establish an EU-wide banking regulatory regime was the "biggest design flaw" of the monetary union when it was set up. There was a lot of debate at the time of interest rates dropping for countries like Ireland and the fact that they'd lose the ability to devalue their currency in times of trouble, but nobody talked about cross-border bank resolution. The monetary union encouraged banks to go across borders and set up shop in other Eurozone countries, but they were left unchecked by local and home-country regulators alike, he says. "Who's going to pay the bills when a bank that's active in multiple countries? That's an unresolved problem."

The 1992 Maastricht Treaty that laid the foundation of the monetary union actually had provisions to give the ECB oversight role on the region's banks, says former Prime Minister Bruton. The statue of the European System of Central Banks that accompanied the treaty had several articles that saw the ECB's role as a macroprudential supervisor, coordinating with member-country central banks to make sure banks in countries where the economy was overheating were reined in.[7] Germany tried to explicitly give such powers to the ECB in the late 1990s, but it was blocked by France, Bruton says. The French thought the ECB was too much of a German institution and didn't want it to have wider supervisory power over the region's banks. If the ECB had this mandate clearly, would it really use it to restrain German banks lending to their Irish counterparts during the country's boom? While deregulation was the order of the day for most of the last two decades in the United States as well as Europe, banking regulators and central banks everywhere still had supervisory powers that could have led to precautionary measures, which they didn't use.

The failure of bank oversight occurred at multiple levels in the EU, not just the result of a disengaged ECB. All the government-commissioned reports looking into Ireland's financial crisis conclude that the country's central bank and the banking regulator, Financial Services Authority (FSA), failed to see the economy's overheating as well as the sector's role and growing risks alongside it.[8] "The regulator was just a cheerleader for a great little banking sector in a great little country," says Minister Burton. "They never asked the question of how a bank can grow 35 percent a year." The FSA didn't regulate the foreign banks that set up shop in the International Financial Services Centre overlooking the River Liffey in Dublin, and neither did their home regulators. When DEPFA, the German Hypo Real Estate's Irish unit, was falling down in 2008, Irish officials were worried that they'd also have to rescue it because it was technically an Irish bank on paper. They were relieved when Germany came to the aid of HRE and thus DEPFA. The incident points to the weakness in oversight in all of Europe though. Banks fell through the cracks because everybody thought it was somebody else's responsibility.

Zombies No More?

Even after €46 billion of new capital from the government, the Irish banks were not resuscitated. In March 2011, the central bank carried out a second stress test to see what additional capital they might need. Like all other bank stress tests, the aim was to convince investors that the banks had enough equity buffers to withstand further losses. The central bank ordered the remaining banks—Anglo Irish, in wind-down mode, was no longer included in the tests—to raise another €24 billion.[9] About half of that was for Allied Irish Bank, most of which the government provided, thereby completing the nationalization of the second largest national lender. Bank of Ireland, the biggest lender, met its €5 billion requirement through a share sale, as well as by asking some of its bond holders to convert debt into stock to prevent falling into state control. By the end of July 2011, the Irish government had injected another €16 billion into its zombie banks, bringing its capital support to €62 billion (Figure 5.2).[10]

The banks aren't out of the doldrums because piecemeal fixes over the past two years have failed to get to the bottom of their problems. They need to be cleaned out completely. All toxic assets need to be put into separate bad banks so future investors and creditors know there will be no more surprise losses to the degree that has emerged since 2008. "Everything we've said about our banks has turned out to be worse, so it won't be easy to restore our reputation," says Minister Burton. Irish authorities did set up a bad bank at the end of 2009, targeting the loans to developers that began to sour before everything else. The National Asset Management Agency (NAMA) took over €71 billion of loans from five banks at an average 58 percent discount (i.e., paying 42 cents on the dollar for each loan). However, NAMA isn't exactly a bad bank. In order to avoid adding the bad debt onto the government balance sheet already strained, Ireland set up NAMA to be majority-owned by private investors. Thus, instead of just taking the toxic stuff, the organization took over all the developer loans above a preset size, good and bad alike. That means the banks have lost some of their best performing loans while still being stuck with smaller nonperforming ones.[11] Some developers whose businesses haven't exploded and are still paying back their loans on

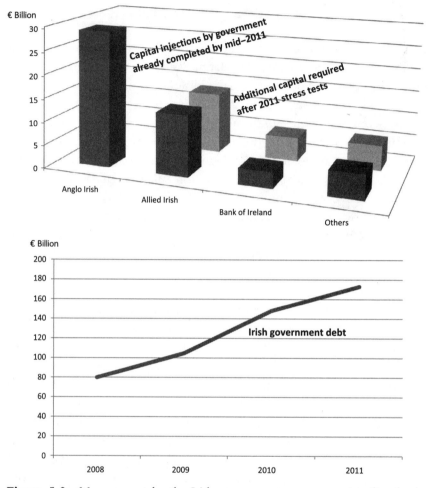

Figure 5.2 Money spent by the Irish government to prop up its ailing banks and the nation's rising public debt. The capital required after 2011 stress tests might not all be provided by the government, as the banks struggle to raise private cash.

SOURCES: National Treasury Management Agency (Ireland), Eurostat, *Financial Times*, *Bloomberg News*.

time have sued NAMA to reverse decisions to take on their debt, arguing that has hurt their reputations. "It's probably the worst model," says Joseph Stiglitz, a Nobel laureate in economics. "The bad bank is buying the good assets at discount prices while the government is left with the bad assets at the supposedly good banks." Stiglitz testified at an Irish court in 2010 in favor of Patrick McKillen, one of those who have sued NAMA. McKillen won his court battle in 2011.[12]

The Crippled Housing Market

There are still about €170 billion of construction, developer, commercial, and real estate loans on the banks' books, in addition to some €120 billion of mortgages. In the March 2011 stress tests, potential losses on those loans were calculated very aggressively, according to the Irish authorities. However, outsiders looking at the central bank's "adverse" scenarios are somewhat skeptical that the worst case has been considered. The housing price decline that's considered in the stressed scenario has already happened; the economic contraction assumed could be much worse; unemployment has already reached what was foreseen as the worst possible outcome, critics say. While the Irish economy contracted by 1 percent in 2010, the adverse case assumes a 0.2 percent shrinking. Unemployment hit 14.7 percent in the first quarter of 2011 whereas the 2011 "stressed" figure is only 14.9 percent.[13] "None of these assumptions are very stressful," says Karl Whelan, an economics professor at University College Dublin. The tests were better than the previous year's exercise, but they still didn't incorporate the worst possible losses, Whelan says. Trinity College's Gurdgiev, who was among a group of academics briefed by the central bank on the tests, says the loss assumptions on mortgages weren't too harsh either and that the differences in the types of outstanding loans weren't taken into account.

Ronán Lyons, an economist who tracks the housing market, says that in rural Ireland, prices don't reflect reality because there are few transactions happening. So even though prices are down about 50 percent from their 2007 peak in places like Dublin, they still look as if they're 20 to 30 percent down in many areas, he says. They need to fall much further before the market can stabilize, according to Lyons. Price-to-income ratios show that the average home price needs to decline by another 30 percent before reaching a normal level, some argue (Figure 5.3). Estimates of the number of homes stuck in ghost estates reach 300,000.[14] Lyons says his estimate of 35,000, though not

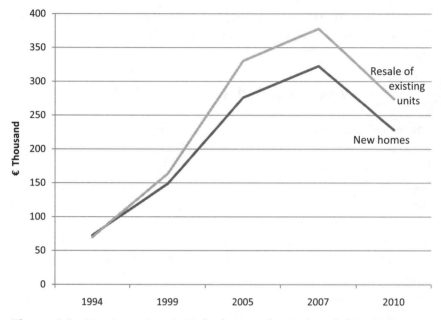

Figure 5.3 Housing prices in Ireland more than quintupled in just over a decade. The roughly 30 percent decline from the peak so far might not be enough, many analysts say.
SOURCE: Department of the Community, Environment and Local Government (Ireland).

as scary, could still take five years to clear, which means prices will be depressed for a while. Even in downtown Dublin, there are plenty of ghost buildings. A stranger looking for an address in the financial district can run into, within the same block, half a dozen newly built, shiny glass towers whose doors are locked shut. Most of those office buildings never got any tenants after being completed around the end of the boom; some closed their doors after the company occupying the tower went bust.

About three-fourths of the mortgages in the country are variable rate ones, based on ECB interest rates. As the ECB raises rates, they will reset higher, causing further difficulties for homeowners' ability to pay, leading to more defaults and further price declines. Studies show that a one percentage point increase in mortgage rates reduces the probability of a housing slump ending by 10 percent.[15] The rising ECB rates also hurt the banks, which rely heavily on borrowing from the central bank. A quarter-point increase in April 2011—from 1 percent to 1.25 percent—increased the banks' borrowing costs by 25 percent, points out Anglo Irish Chairman Dukes. The ECB raised its rates by another quarter point in July 2011 to 1.5 percent.

The banks cannot come out of the hole until their balance sheets are fully cleansed of troubled loans and mortgages, according to Dukes. "Cleanup means crystallizing chunky losses, and government doesn't have the money to do that," he says, contrasting the slow pace of tackling problems in his home country to Iceland's speedy cleanup of its banking system. Dukes recalls how the same slow approach was favored in the 1980s when Ireland faced fiscal problems. As finance minister, Dukes argued that the fix should be done fast and pain taken upfront, but his colleagues didn't heed his view and took the slow road, which extended the pain for several years and cost them the next elections.

Will the Tiger Make It?

Dukes calculates the full debt burden on the taxpayer for the banks' cleanup to be roughly €200 billion. The country can perhaps pay half of that in the next 10 years, he says. The other half has to be written off or spread over many decades to avoid a default, according to Dukes. "You can make slaves out of Irish people, but they still can't pay that back," says Socialist politician Higgins. Sarah Carey, a former columnist for the *Sunday Times* and *Irish Times* newspapers, says there will likely be a default in two years because the country cannot afford to pay, and, by then, Germany and France expect their banks to be healthy enough to absorb the losses. Irish government officials insist the country can pay. Ireland has made harsh fiscal adjustments in the past (such as in the 1980s) and can pull this one off too, they say. The Kenny government has been trying to get the interest rate on its EU-IMF loans reduced, but Germany has objected, demanding that Ireland bump up its corporate tax rate, the lowest in the union, in return for a rate cut. The low tax rate has helped Ireland attract foreign investment from global giants like Google, and increasing it would destroy its economy, the Irish say. "If Germany and France force higher corporate tax, we'll have to turn ECB debt into equity in the banks," says economist Lyons.

As in the case of Greece, austerity measures trying to cut the government budget deficit also hurt the chances of economic recovery and make it harder for Ireland to pay back. The impact of the three-year-old recession can be seen even better in poorer areas of Dublin, where shuttered storefronts sometimes fill up a whole block and "To Let" signs on houses and apartments are too numerous to count. Restaurant managers, storeowners, and salaried employees all make the same complaints: business is slow and taxes are higher, making it really hard to go on. Despite the setbacks, Ireland is multiple times better off than it was a few decades ago, says former Prime Minister Bruton. In the 1950s, when he was growing up in Dunboyne, a small town half an hour west of Dublin, there were kids who were going to school with no shoes on, Bruton recalls. Now there's a train station, and even Lebanese and Chinese restaurants in his hometown. "We can afford the wealth to decline a little, so long as this burden is distributed fairly," says Bruton. "This may require more progressive taxation as well as expenditure reductions."

The "Germans," that is, the IMF team, initially questioned why they were in Ireland because downtown Dublin looked so prosperous and like any other Western European city. Being used to setting up camp in the capitals of emerging economies that go bust often, many with incomplete infrastructure and visible poverty on main streets, the team members went through a culture shock at first. Ireland is clearly no developing country as it was in the 1950s, but there's also no doubt that the Irish need to pay for the sins they committed during the latest boom years, which were a bubble, by giving up some of their comforts. But the numbers don't add up if only they are to sacrifice while the German and/or French taxpayers are to be spared completely. Irish banks, companies, and consumers borrowed irresponsibly, but German and French banks lent the same way. So the pain needs to be shared by both sides. Meanwhile, Ireland has more to do to clean up its zombie banks, just like its EU partners.

Chapter 6

The Reincarnation of Iceland's Banks

When Iceland's authorities seized the country's three main banks in October 2008, they struggled at first to keep things running. The banks' creditors, depositors, banks in other countries, clearing agencies—everybody panicked. They didn't know what it meant for a country's whole banking system to collapse (the three accounted for 87 percent of the nation's financial assets). "Nobody wanted to work with an Icelandic bank," says one of the bank executives appointed by the authorities after the takeover. The overseas assets of the banks were frozen in several countries, the United Kingdom going as far as using antiterrorist laws to do so. Even though the Icelandic government had issued a guarantee on domestic deposits, people flocked to ATMs to withdraw money. Arni Tomasson, who was asked to oversee one of the banks, remembers how he scrambled to find cash to fill up the ATMs after a rash of withdrawals spurred by a delayed public announcement on the banks' situation. "We were all trying to make sure life could go on as normal, that people could use their credit cards, get their salaries, companies could transfer money," Tomasson says.

Despite all the difficulties and panic, Tomasson and others managed to keep the banks functioning. And within two weeks, the government announced it was setting up new banks with clean balance sheets, leaving the troubled assets and losses with the old banks. Resolution committees would sift through those and deal with the claims of the creditors while the new banks could move on with their regular business.

The panic about Iceland's banks, whose assets had grown to 11 times the national economy, started at the same time as Ireland's lenders. After Lehman Brothers' bankruptcy on September 15, both countries' banks ran into funding problems because they had over-reached, and the world knew that. On September 29, when the Irish government decided to guarantee all its banks' liabilities, Iceland decided to buy a 75 percent stake in the country's third biggest lender. However, a week later, when troubles spread to the other two banks, Iceland went exactly in the opposite direction of its oceanic neighbor 900 miles to the southeast. The government pushed through parliament an emergency law that gave it powers to seize the banks, restructure them, and guarantee only domestic deposits. So while one island's banks were kept alive as zombies for two more years before they brought down the whole country with them, the neighboring island's troubled banks were allowed to die. Their reincarnations emerged quickly as smaller, more focused, and cleaned-up versions of their former selves to support Iceland's economic recovery.

To be fair, in addition to the similarities between their situations, Ireland and Iceland had several key differences that cannot be overlooked. Iceland wasn't part of the Eurozone and had an independent currency that it could devalue when trouble struck. Even with their overgrown size, Iceland's banking sector was about one-third the size of the Irish domestic banks (Ireland didn't rescue the subsidiaries of foreign lenders domiciled in Dublin). Therefore, the losses faced by the creditors of the Icelandic institutions were more manageable. Yet these weren't impediments to Ireland taking a similar path to Iceland when their banks ran into trouble. The devaluation of the Icelandic currency, the krona, didn't solve that island's problems overnight whereas Ireland has been cutting wages, increasing taxes, and implementing other measures that are mimicking the outcome of a devalued currency. Europe's banks, pension funds, and insurance companies could handle the default of Irish banks just as they handled Icelandic losses. "Ireland's banks were not too big to fail either," says Adriaan van der Knaap, a UBS managing director who advises governments on bank restructuring.

The Land of Fire and Ice Catches Fire

Iceland is known as the land of fire and ice because some of Europe's largest glaciers rub elbows with the continent's largest volcanoes on the same island. Separated from the nearest land mass by the rough seas of the North Atlantic Ocean, in perpetual darkness for half the year (well, you do get a few hours of dusk in the middle of the day), and most of it uninhabited due to ice or fire, Iceland's population lingers around 300,000, give or take a few thousand depending on that year's migration trend. The story of how this island caught financial fire is in a lot of ways similar to its distant neighbor, Ireland: free money sloshing around the world in the early 2000s, the meteoric rise of its banks binging on that money, and a housing boom supported by the first two.

Just as the U.S. Federal Reserve started cutting interest rates after the dot-com bubble burst and the European Central Bank (ECB) followed suit, Iceland sold its majority stakes in the two largest banks in 2002. A year later, the government lowered how much down payment home buyers had to make, allowing 90 percent loan-to-value ratio in purchases. So the newly privatized banks, along with the third bank already in private hands, started feasting on the cheap loans from the German, French, and British banks to manage a sevenfold increase in their assets between 2000 and 2008 (Figure 6.1). Banking's share of national output almost doubled to 9 percent, whereas that of fishing, the traditional backbone of Iceland's economy, was halved to 4 percent. The profit of the number-one bank, Kaupthing, surged 100-fold to almost $1 billion. With 80 percent home ownership and 2 percent unemployment, the Icelandic people were pretty well off even before the bonanza started. They still gorged on the cheap credit, expanding the size of their homes and their cars, buying second or

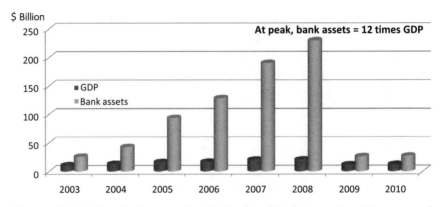

Figure 6.1 Iceland's fast-growing banks dwarfed their nation. Here, annual gross domestic product is compared to the total assets of the nation's commercial banks. 2008 data is midyear figure to show the peak before the banks' collapse later that year.
SOURCES: Financial Supervisory Authority (Iceland), Statistics Iceland.

third homes. More homes were built from 2004 to 2008 than in the entire previous decade, while prices almost doubled.[1]

And yet the small island's already wealthy population wasn't enough to satisfy the appetites of the growing banks. So they turned overseas, making loans to property developers in England and the United States, and companies in Denmark and Norway. Kaupthing's lending outside Iceland reached three-fourths of its loan book. So how could a small island's internationally unknown banks grab market share from those countries' powerful, much bigger banks? They were either lending to firms that the local banks had passed up or to Icelandic businessmen who went on a buying spree on the continent. The acquisitions abroad were at high prices and fully funded by debt, which made them riskier and easier to go sour when the global economy turned downward, according to Gunnar T. Andersen, head of the country's banking regulator. "Excessive risk-taking, greed and ambition were always three steps ahead of capability," says Andersen, who was appointed after the collapse. The agency he took over was underfunded and understaffed to properly supervise the incredibly fast growing financial institutions, Andersen adds.

There was also a lot of related lending, to directors of the banks and their companies. British entrepreneur Robert Tchenguiz—who indirectly owned the biggest stake in Kaupthing—and firms with ties to him accounted for a quarter of the bank's loans. Tchenguiz and his brother were arrested briefly in March 2011 in connection with a fraud investigation the UK authorities are conducting. The Tchenguiz brothers claim they have done nothing illegal.[2] The companies with weak collateral and the Icelandic consumers who overreached because of the mistaken belief they were richer as their currency appreciated were the "subprime borrowers" of Iceland's banks, says Magnus Arni Skulason, founder of Reykjavik Economics, a consulting firm. The banks established subsidiaries in other European countries, even collected deposits from some (the United Kingdom, Netherlands, Germany) by offering higher rates to savers. Those overseas operations escaped the attention of banking supervisors on the island, Andersen says. They weren't on the radar screens of UK or Dutch regulators either.

The Unheeded Fire Alarm

There were a few warnings in late 2005 and early 2006 about the dangerous path the country's banks were on. David Oddsson, the longest serving prime minister of the country, became the central-bank governor in October 2005. Two months later, he relayed his concerns about the banks' surging growth to government leaders, he says. The three banks—Kaupthing was followed closely by number-two Landsbanki Islands and number-three Glitnir—had become the largest companies in the country, created thousands of well-paying jobs, took charge of the top trade associations, and were paying the biggest chunk of the taxes, Oddsson says. "So nobody wanted to listen when the party was on," he says. After recognizing the threat, Oddsson could build the central bank's foreign currency reserves to prepare for a possible bailout of the lenders, but he claims to have chosen not to do so because "it would be stupid" to rescue them. Oddsson jacked up interest rates to slow down the housing and consumption frenzy fueled by the lending, but the banks got around that by making loans in foreign currency, for which they could charge less because they were borrowing it at a lower rate from German banks. Oddsson may have woken up to the dangers of the growing banks, but he wasn't as innocent as it sounds either. As prime minister until 2004, he led the privatization of the two largest banks. A series of articles in the *Frettabladid* newspaper at the time reported that Oddsson and his finance minister Geir Haarde manipulated the sales process so their close supporters would get the largest stakes.[3] Haarde was the prime minister Oddsson was alerting about the banks a few years later.

Another warning came from Fitch Ratings, which placed the country's credit rating on negative watch in February 2006, followed by analyst reports raising concern on the Icelandic banks. While those increased the banks' borrowing costs in European markets, they turned to the United States, where money was still cheap and nobody really paid attention to what was included in a collateralized debt obligation as long as it was rated high investment grade. So Icelandic bank debt was packaged into collateralized debt obligations (CDOs), sold in the United States, and gave the banks new sources of funding to continue their frenzy.[4] And again, nobody heeded the warnings.

Whether Oddsson had acted intentionally or not, by the time the banks blew up, the country didn't have the means to rescue them. The central bank didn't have the foreign currency to back their liabilities, and not being part of the Eurozone, there was no ECB to turn to either. So when the banks couldn't roll over their debt at the end of September 2008, the government had to let them fail. They'd gotten too big to save while other countries such as the United States and Ireland rushed to the aid of their too-big-to-fail banks. With the emergency act passed by Parliament on October 6, the government seized the three top lenders. Their assets and liabilities were split based on whether they were originated at home or abroad. The three new banks, also created by the legislation, were given the domestic deposits and loans made to Icelandic companies and consumers. Resolution committees were set up to manage and liquidate what the old banks were left with: the overseas borrowing and lending. As a result, German lenders, such as Dekabank, the asset management firm of the savings banks, were left holding the bag along with London-based hedge funds, European pension funds, and other creditors.

Devaluation No Panacea

When Iceland's housing/banking bubble burst, the overvalued currency came tumbling down, losing 58 percent of its value in two months after the banks' seizure. Inflation spiked to 19 percent a few months later.[5] That led to a serious economic recession and a surge in unemployment. Although the devaluation of the currency made Iceland's exports more competitive in world markets, there was too much consumer and corporate debt that was denominated in foreign currencies, so the drop in krona's value made those balloon and led to a surge of bankruptcies. What devaluation has done in Iceland almost overnight—cut the wealth of the island's population by half—austerity measures in the EU periphery countries are trying to do slowly through tax increases, benefit reductions, and government job cuts. Still, being swift and less politically controversial doesn't make a currency devaluation any less painful. And it doesn't create a sharp economic recovery just like that either. "Having an independent currency you can devalue is a double-edged sword," says Árni Páll Árnason, Iceland's minister of economic affairs. "Of course it helped exports but it also hurt households. Wealth is cut; purchasing power is reduced. These have hampered recovery. It's hard to generate growth when you have excessive debt levels for households and corporations." To cushion the krona's drop, the government also implemented capital controls, restricting the outflow of foreign currency deposits and investments in the country. Those still haven't been lifted completely, though they've been eased. That also makes foreign investors edgy about reinvesting in Iceland and the new banks less able to manage their currency risks.

Even with the 58 percent devaluation, the economic devastation in Iceland has been less harsh than in Ireland. Unemployment rose to only 8 percent, about half of Ireland's 15 percent. While both countries' economies contracted by about 10 percent since the crisis, the International Monetary Fund (IMF) expects Iceland to grow by 2.3 percent in 2011, but another year of stagnation is forecast in Ireland. Of course, the most striking part of the differences in the two islands' experiences result from their opposing treatments of the failing banks. Ireland's debt is already almost 100 percent of gross domestic product

(GDP) and expected to go up to 120 whereas Iceland's peaked at 85 and is declining (Figure 6.2).[6] Also, the figures for Ireland don't include the toxic assets taken on by the bad bank the government set up because it's technically majority owned by private investors. Because it's thinly capitalized, the losses from the bad bank will also fall on the shoulders of the Irish taxpayer at the end. Meanwhile, the Icelandic

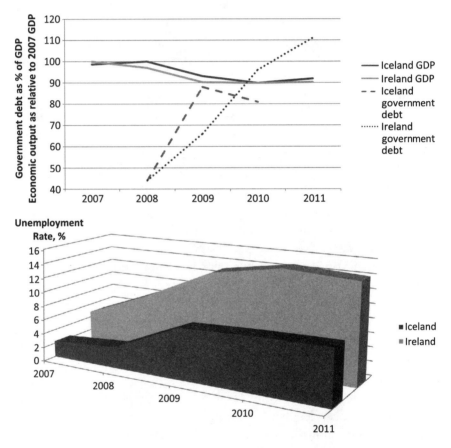

Figure 6.2 Comparison of Ireland's and Iceland's economic contractions, rising debt, and unemployment levels. 2011 economic growth based on IMF estimates; 2011 unemployment figures as of first quarter for Iceland and as of May for Ireland; 2011 Ireland debt estimate by the Irish government, no estimate available for Iceland.

SOURCES: OECD, National Treasury Management Agency (Ireland), Statistics Iceland, Central Statistics Office Ireland, International Monetary Fund.

taxpayer is immune from the bad banks' losses. Almost everyone in Iceland sighs in relief looking at Ireland. "There's no bottom to banks' losses," says Economy Minister Árnason. Höskuldur Ólafsson, who runs Arion Banki, one of the new banks, says not guaranteeing the failed lenders' liabilities saved Iceland. "Our future isn't as bleak because our public debt isn't as high," he says.

Good Bank–Bad Bank, Sort of . . .

Because Iceland wanted to separate its bust banks' overseas adventures from their homeland activities, the split of assets and liabilities wasn't in the tradition of good bank-bad bank exactly. There were plenty of toxic loans, including Iceland-style subprime mortgages, made at home that ended up on the new banks' balance sheets. But they were transferred from the old banks with serious haircuts depending on the likelihood of repayment, sometimes at zero valuations. So even though the new banks have been involved in a nationwide restructuring effort to improve recovery, they have had enough of a margin on the valuations to offer companies or homeowners reductions on their principal. That's what has been missing from the Irish or U.S. experiences, which has prevented the housing markets from recovering. Because zombie banks cannot afford to make reductions on their bad loans, the clearing of the housing glut is delayed while the zombies try to earn enough to cover such losses. "Iceland cleaned out its banks; we decided to spread it over time," says Alan Dukes, the new chairman of Anglo Irish bank tasked with winding down the first lender to go bust in Ireland.

The managements of the new Icelandic banks completed the restructuring of corporate loans on their books in 2010 and were hoping to finish the process with thousands of home and consumer loans in 2011 though the IMF has indicated the process is going more slowly than expected.[7] Still, the new banks—Arion Banki, Islandsbanki, and NBI—made a combined profit of $600 million in 2010.[8] The profitability of the banks is important because the goal is to sell them in three to five years. Arion and Islandsbanki are owned by the creditors to the old banks, who will get the upshot of their improving prospects through better sale prices. NBI has a promissory note to the creditors, whose value will increase if the bank does well. The banks are hoping to return to international capital markets to borrow again as well, to diversify their sources of funding and make them more appealing to potential buyers. The prospects of that are also improving as the country's economy improves, along with the banks' profits. "In the beginning, banks and other financial institutions in Europe were telling us, 'Never again will we lend to you,'" says Islandsbanki CEO Birna Einarsdóttir. "Then it was 10 years, then 5. Now they say they might soon be ready to lend again."

One thing that has clouded the picture for the banks and the country's credit worthiness has been an international dispute over the payment of deposits collected by one of the old banks overseas. Although they all enticed deposits (mostly through online banking) in other countries, the biggest operation was by Landsbanki, which ended up hoarding about $5 billion from British and Dutch savers under the online scheme Icesave.

The Icesave Saga

The TV commercials for Icesave boasted of the savings accounts' transparency (because it paid high interest rates without any conditions attached) without ever explaining how it was possible that it could pay such higher rates. When Iceland's emergency act in October 2008 didn't include overseas deposits in the government's guarantee, the United Kingdom and Netherlands took it upon themselves to pay the depositors in their own countries and then demanded full payment from the Icelandic state. Iceland agreed to pay the $5 billion back, but the independent president, Olafur Ragnar Grimsson, who has very little power except rejecting legislation and demanding a referendum, did so twice regarding the payments to the United Kingdom and Netherlands. Both times the people voted down the proposed payback, even though the second time around the government had negotiated very easy payments spread over 35 years. Those campaigning against the payments have argued that it's not the debt of the nation but of private banks that had private owners and creditors.[9]

The government of Iceland has been hoping all along to cover the payments to the other two countries through the liquidation of Landsbanki's assets. German banks and other creditors have been disputing the legality of the 2008 emergency act, which had put all deposits ahead of other liabilities in the hierarchy of payments during the resolution process. They have been arguing that they loaned to Landsbanki long before the act changed the payment order and that deposits should be in line like everybody else. In April 2011, Icelandic courts sided with the government, upholding the emergency law's hierarchy. If the appeals court upholds the lower courts' decision to allow depositors to remain on top of the payments from the liquidation, UK and Dutch governments would be first in line to get their money back from the estate of Landsbanki. That would cover the Icesave payments in full. Other investors would pretty much get nothing then. If they all share the proceeds from asset sales, then the ratio would be roughly 30 percent recovery for all. That's close to the recovery rate for the other two banks.[10]

The Icesave saga points to a crucial weakness in global banking: the lack of rules on cross-border resolution. So it's not only the Eurozone countries that haven't thought of how to regulate their banks as the financial system integrated and more lenders did more business across borders. The world's banks have gone increasingly international in the last two decades, but regulation and oversight have lagged far behind. While regulators worldwide have paid lip service to cooperation, they were pretty much unaware of their home-country banks' operations in other countries or operations of other countries' banks in their own territory. As was the case with Ireland's international banking center, everybody thought somebody else was taking care of the oversight. So when the Icelandic banks blew up and their activities in other European countries had to be wound down, too, there were no mechanisms to do it in an orderly fashion, and every country grabbed what it could. Since the 2008 global financial crisis, there has been more discussion of a cross-border scheme though efforts to create one have been fruitless so far.[11]

The unresolved dispute over Icesave slowed Iceland's efforts to regain its credibility in financial markets. The government had to delay plans to sell international bonds. The court decisions in favor of the government on the priority of deposits in the liquidation process eased the concerns to a great extent because it will allow the resolution committees of the old banks to pay England and the Netherlands through the liquidation of assets. In June 2011, Iceland managed to sell its first international bond since the crisis. The $1 billion bond sale was oversubscribed, investors seeking to buy twice as much as what was being offered for sale.[12]

Reincarnation and Recovery

Clearly, Iceland's path hasn't been that smooth since 2008. Yet the land of fire and ice has done several things correctly, which are now easing its return to normalcy. First, it didn't convert the private debts of its banks to public as Ireland did. The creditors of the banks— German lenders as well as other European investors—have thus shared the costs of the gamble that went wrong, along with the Icelandic people. That has also spared Iceland the incredible debt burden that has made Ireland's sovereign solvency questionable. So Iceland could start its economic recovery whereas the periphery countries cannot due to the debt overhang, says Desmond Lachman, a scholar at the American Enterprise Institute for Public Policy Research in Washington. Iceland's currency has recouped some of its losses; inflation has come down to 3 percent and economic growth has resumed slowly.

Second, it didn't prop up the failed banks and allow them to live as zombies. The full clean-up of the balance sheets, through a mixture of good bank-bad bank split, serious write-downs and debt restructurings, have made the new banks viable, profitable, and able to stand on their own feet without any government support. They can be sold soon whereas the half-completed cleanup of German or Irish zombies renders their sale impossible. "New Icelandic banks are clean while most European banks aren't still," says UBS's Van der Knaap, who has advised Iceland's banks in their restructuring efforts. Van der Knaap suspects the resistance to letting banks fail in the rest of Europe is over concern that banks' borrowing costs would rise considerably going forward if bondholders are burned. But perhaps their borrowing costs have been too low, not taking the risks into account properly, and perhaps they should go up to reflect the risks—such as lending billions to land developers during a housing boom.

Ireland and Iceland have both suffered in the last few years. The biggest fear of the politicians on both islands is how much outward migration that suffering may cause. Both nations have a history of such outflows and are worried about losing their best educated, talented people when times get tough. Net migration has been over 40,000 from Ireland in 2009–2010, the biggest since the 1980s. Iceland has seen some 7,000 people leave in that period. Having a much smaller population, Iceland's outward migration accounts for 2 percent while Ireland's is half that.[13] Yet, Iceland's slowed in 2010 while Ireland's picked up pace, another sign of the diverging paths of the two countries' future prospects. The return of Iceland to international capital markets in mid-2011 put it ahead of Ireland by several years too. Nobel laureate Joseph Stiglitz says the opposing approaches the two took to treating their zombies is the key to the divergence now. "Iceland is a success story," he says. "It has managed to turn the worst crisis to recovery."

Chapter 7

U.S. Zombies on
IV Drip

A t the time Ireland's leaders were deciding to offer a blanket
guarantee for their banks' liabilities, U.S. officials were also
discussing measures to stem the panic in financial markets
following the collapse of Lehman Brothers. The idea of a blanket
guarantee was first brought up by Timothy Geithner, head of the
New York Federal Reserve at the time, during the summer of 2008
but was dismissed as too radical by others. However, a few months
later and after Lehman's fall in September, it was back on the table
and its proponents had grown in number. This time Treasury Secretary
Henry Paulson and Fed Chairman Ben Bernanke were also leaning
toward supporting it, hoping that it would help reverse the erosion
of trust in the banking system.

Two days after Iceland's parliament passed its emergency act to
seize its banks, a memo from Paulson's office proposed a public statement that would announce the U.S. authorities' full support to "protect
depositors, protect unsecured claims, guarantee liabilities and adopt
other measures to support the banking system." Not everybody liked
the idea. Sheila Bair, chairman of the Federal Deposit Insurance

Corporation (FDIC), didn't think the guarantee was warranted. She wrote a long response to Paulson and Bernanke—starting with "Dear Hank and Ben"—explaining why it wasn't. Bair told her colleagues that the guarantee would encourage banks to borrow more rather than raise capital and insolvent banks to attempt growing out of their problems. She suggested instead that the Treasury use Troubled Asset Relief Program (TARP) funds authorized by Congress to inject capital into banks, that the government offer guarantees on new bank debt to be issued for a temporary period and insure some banks' certain group of assets against further losses.[1]

Though it came close, Bair's arguments won the day, and the United States ended up not going Ireland's way. A blanket guarantee for all bank liabilities would have potentially caused the U.S. government debt to swell by $5.6 trillion, or about 40 percent of national output. The measures taken, some of which were suggested by Bair, cost about $1 trillion, most of which has since been recovered.[2] But even though the United States didn't repeat Ireland's big mistake, it didn't follow in Iceland's footsteps either. The biggest troubled banks that were on the verge of death at the peak of the crisis weren't seized and liquidated. Instead, they were patched up with capital infusions, temporary debt, and asset guarantees, and allowed to live as zombies like Germany's were. Despite Bair's warning in October 2008, they have been allowed to try growing out of their troubles.

The Fed's zero percent interest rates maintained years after the crisis and its efforts to prop up the housing market have been like IV drips that slowly are nursing the banks back to health, along with regulatory forbearance that overlooks their unrecognized losses. Even though there was some discussion of nationalizing the largest troubled banks, Bair's opinion wasn't sought on that. Three years later, on her way out of office, Bair says it was rather murky whether nationalization was possible within the legal framework of the time. The FDIC could seize banks, but the toxic assets were housed in the bank-holding companies, technically out of the FDIC's reach. "I'm sympathetic to people who wanted to nationalize the banks, but it wasn't clear to me how you'd do that," Bair says. Of course, the U.S. Congress could pass emergency legislation the way Iceland did to make it happen if it came to that. But it never did.

Her resistance to the blanket guarantee almost cost Bair her job. Geithner, picked by president-elect Barack Obama to be his Treasury Secretary, tried to have the FDIC chairman replaced when the new administration was preparing to take the reins in January 2009. Bair, appointed in 2006 by President George W. Bush, had been asked by Obama to stay on as the new Democratic leader tried to include Republicans in his administration to fulfill his campaign promise of reaching across the aisle. Geithner's campaign through media leaks[3] to oust Bair backfired and made her allies within the Democratic ranks rally for support. Barney Frank and Christopher Dodd, the influential Democratic chairmen of House and Senate financial-services committees at the time, asked Obama to keep Bair, as did Rahm Emanuel, Obama's first chief of staff. So she stayed, causing more headaches for Geithner, who has consistently taken the banks' side on issues ranging from whether to nationalize them to toughening regulations on them.

Saving Citi—Again

Another big reason behind Geithner's efforts to get Bair removed was their repeated clashes over the rescue operations to save Citigroup in late 2008 and early 2009. Citi, the second largest U.S. bank by assets then, had the biggest losses worldwide during the crisis as its oversized bets on subprime mortgages and complicated securities based on those blew up. Citi started racking up losses in the fall of 2007, as cracks in the U.S. subprime market first appeared. Initially it was able to find capital from sovereign wealth funds and other investors, but after Bear Stearns' fire-sale in March 2008 and as things started to get worse for the whole housing market, such funding dried up and its creditors started to shy away from renewing short-term loans as well.[4] After Lehman's fall, those fears increased, and Citi was fast approaching the end of its life.

This wasn't Citi's first near-death experience either: In 1992, when real estate losses at home and abroad brought it to the verge of collapse, Citi was saved by a capital injection from Saudi Prince Alwaleed bin Talal and the Fed's massive interest-rate cuts.[5] Prince Alwaleed tried to save Citi again in 2008 by announcing he would increase his stake in the bank, but this time the loss of confidence and the hole in the balance sheet were much larger. Therefore, the U.S. government had to come to the rescue, and not just with interest-rate cuts.

On September 29, the day Ireland's leaders huddled in a room to make their disastrous blanket-guarantee decision, Citigroup announced that it was buying Wachovia, a smaller troubled bank faced with massive mortgage losses and a run on its uninsured deposits.[6] Although the sale was publicized as an effort to save Wachovia, it was really to save Citi, people involved in the discussions at the time say. FDIC's Bair was planning to seize Wachovia and wind it down, but Geithner had other plans: to use it as cover to help stabilize Citi. The global conglomerate with most of its deposits outside the United States (and thus not FDIC insured) would get another $448 billion of domestic deposits, quadrupling its FDIC-backed deposit base, the most stable funding source. The regulator would also provide a guarantee against losses on the most toxic assets of Wachovia. There was also an attempt to include some of Citi's most toxic stuff in the guaranteed stuff, but Bair wouldn't allow that. Even without the last part, the Wachovia deal was an effort to rescue Citigroup silently as much as it was to find a home for the collapsing domestic lender.

So when Wells Fargo, the fourth largest U.S. bank, announced a competing bid for Wachovia that didn't involve any government support, Geithner wasn't happy. He wanted the Citi-Wachovia deal to go through. Bair, who had reluctantly agreed to that anyway, was in favor of Wells Fargo's acquisition because it wouldn't put the FDIC—and thus the taxpayer, because FDIC's holes are covered by the U.S. Treasury—on the hook for any potential future losses. Bair wanted Wachovia shareholders to make the decision. Wells Fargo was also offering a higher share price than Citi was, so Wachovia's shareholders opted for the superior one. "Tim and I were at complete loggerheads over Citi, absolutely at each other hammer and tongs," recalls Bair.

She might have won this round, but Geithner prevailed in successive efforts to rescue the bank. Geithner, let's not forget, was a protégé of Robert Rubin at the Treasury in the early 1990s and Rubin left office to work for Citi and was an executive at the bank until January 2009. Citi received two injections of capital from the government totaling $45 billion as well as a guarantee on some $300 billion of its assets. The funds it got from the government were much higher than its market value at the time, so in a way it was nationalized. However, true nationalization would have meant a change of management, being split into good bank-bad bank like those in Iceland and eventual breakup. Geithner didn't do any of those. Instead, even as the $141 billion of losses wiped out its equity,[7] Citi's shareholders were protected and allowed to benefit from a partial recovery in the share price thanks to the government's obvious stance that it would never let the firm die.

A Snake Gobbling Up Poisoned Rats

Even though it also grew into prominence with a series of mergers like the ones that Sandy Weill put together to build Citi, Bank of America's history had lacked big blowups and government rescues. But the latest two acquisitions it made would change that. Just as the U.S. subprime crisis was brewing in January 2008, the bank bought Countrywide Financial, the largest mortgage lender in the United States and among the top subprime loan providers. As the crisis entered its most critical phase with the collapse of Lehman Brothers, Bank of America purchased Merrill Lynch, an investment bank that was the top underwriter of complex securities tied to the housing market and was reeling from losses on the toxic stuff stuck on its books when the music stopped. While those purchases catapulted Bank of America to number-one bank by assets, it also helped it lose $112 billion—the second worst after Citigroup—and forced it to seek a bailout from the government with three capital injections totaling $45 billion.[8] Again the money put in was as big as the market value of the bank at the time. Not only did the acquired firms bring hundreds of billions of dollars in troubled assets onto the bank's balance sheet, former CEO Kenneth D. Lewis also paid top dollar for the firms at a time when capital was so desperately needed to cover losses.

Lewis tried to back out of the Merrill acquisition a few months after announcing it when the losses at the investment bank swelled beyond Bank of America's initial projections, but he was told by former Treasury Secretary Paulson that he should stick to it and that the government would back Lewis's bank if necessary.[9] Two of the capital injections were made following that conversation. Merrill's accumulation of collateralized debt obligations, mortgage-backed securities, and other bets on the housing market that went sour caused massive losses for Bank of America in early 2009. The losses from Countrywide's home-loan portfolio are still hurting, bleeding slowly as the U.S. housing market wobbles three years on.

What saved both Citi and Bank of America from death, in addition to capital injections, debt, and asset guarantees, as well as suspension of accounting rules, were stress tests carried out in April–May 2009. Unlike the EU's tests that failed to restore confidence in that continent's financial system, the U.S. stress tests were successful in turning around sentiment. The tests were Geithner's idea and even some of his critics credit him for their success. Geithner achieved what his European counterparts failed to because of several factors. First, the criteria used in the tests were much harsher, and the 19 banks included were asked to raise $75 billion in a few months. Citi complied by converting its hybrid capital to equity at very attractive prices. Bank of America was able to sell shares because the extent of its troubles weren't as obvious yet. Second, the U.S. government said it wouldn't let any of the 19 lenders fail, that it would provide the necessary capital if they couldn't find it in the marketplace. That pretty much turned the top U.S. banks into government-backed entities, similar to the status of the mortgage giants Freddie Mac and Fannie Mae before they collapsed—not officially government sponsored, but implicitly the United States wouldn't let them fail. The two have been in government conservatorship since 2008. The implicit support for the largest U.S. banks is included in their credit ratings: Bank of America gets five levels of uplift whereas Citigroup gets four from Moody's Investors Service, a rating agency. In other words, without the backing, Moody's would rate them Baa2, which is barely investment grade. The government backing lifts them up to Aa3 and A1, respectively, giving them cheaper funding in the markets than they'd get otherwise.[10]

The third factor that contributed to the turnaround after the stress tests was the monetary-policy support from the Federal Reserve that gave the U.S. banks almost free money to replenish their coffers and protected the housing market from further declines, so the assumptions for adverse scenarios turned out to be realistic. If the housing market was left to its own means and not propped up, the losses would have been much greater and U.S. tests too optimistic, like their EU counterparts. "Zero interest rate helps banks rebuild capital," says Thomas M. Hoenig, who has been the lonely voice in the Fed against keeping it so low for so long. The banks can borrow from the central bank at close to zero percent, lend to the Treasury at 3 percent, and keep the difference with no effort or risk to make money. The Fed also bought $1.3 trillion of mortgages in an effort to keep interest rates on home lending down. It has purchased another $1 trillion of Treasury bonds as part of its quantitative easing—that is, what a central bank does to ease monetary policy further after it hits the zero percent interest-rate mark. In addition, through the rescue of Fannie and Freddie, the government prevented losses in hundreds of billions of dollars the banks would incur on their holdings of the two giants' debt and mortgage securities.

"Pretend and Extend"

All those efforts have helped the banks recover slowly while the economy has lingered, unemployment stuck at record levels. Banks have not been lending out the money they've been getting; instead, they have been investing in Treasuries or building their spare reserves at the Fed.[11] Joseph Stiglitz, Columbia University professor and winner of the 2001 Nobel Prize in Economics, says the banks prefer to keep credit tight so they can charge higher rates to borrowers and earn money to cover losses as their balance sheets continue to bleed. They also opt for securities trading, which is riskier but more profitable and doesn't necessarily support economic growth, according to Stiglitz. Some of the Fed's quantitative easing has also found its way to emerging markets, where interest rates are higher, creating new bubbles and inflation in places like Brazil and China. "Trading instead of lending is basically gambling for resurrection by zombies," he says, echoing the words of Boston College professor Edward J. Kane on what the U.S. thrifts did in the 1980s. Bank of America has relied on profits from its Merrill Lynch division as its bank side suffers, and Citigroup has ramped up the hiring of traders to boost its income from such activities.[12] The government's efforts to slow housing foreclosures, the temporary first-time homebuyers credit, and other measures all kept the housing market afloat, pushing the day of reckoning off to the future. "It's in a lot of people's interest to pretend and extend, and you never can tell how long you can do that," says Stiglitz.

One pillar of the pretend-and-extend policy—as in other instances of regulatory forbearance exhibited toward zombie banks in history— was softening accounting rules and delaying the implementation of capital regulations. Early on in the crisis, the Financial Accounting Standards Board (FASB), like its counterparts that set accounting rules in Europe, suspended regulations that would force banks to recognize losses on their loans and assets immediately. Banks moved loans or securities to their so-called banking books to avoid marking them to market values even as prices for such assets tumbled. Citigroup moved $13 billion of such toxic assets back to the trading book in April 2011 to sell them slowly, taking a $709 million charge against earnings— which shows that there are still lots of assets that are valued above their market prices and the banks are allowed to hide the losses until they sell them.[13] That reduces their appetite to sell toxic stuff. "Banks aren't selling anything bad because they would have to admit much bigger losses if they did," says James G. Rickards, an advisor to fund managers. "There are willing buyers at 55 cents on the dollar, but they'd rather keep it at 95 cents on the balance sheet. Because they can't get rid of their bad loans and securities, they can't lend more either and end up clogging up the economy."

FASB Chairman Robert H. Herz actually tried to reverse his agency's crisis-time softening on valuing loans and securities once the worst was over. Herz proposed new valuation rules that would be even tougher than before the meltdown, to make sure investors would know what the value of toxic assets were. But the proposal came under extensive attack from his counterparts in Europe and the banks, and Herz was pushed out of his job in October 2010. The lobbying to reverse the attempted strengthening of the valuation standards got more intense after his departure. Two-thirds of the letters sent to FASB during the public comment period opposed the change, according to insiders. CFA Institute, which represents thousands of analysts and fund managers worldwide and was supportive of Herz's initiative, got suspicious of the opposition voiced by investors and decided to investigate. The institute realized a lot of the so-called investors were treasurers of small banks around the country, who invest their bank's funds in stocks and bonds. CFA staff started calling around some of these treasurers and asking them why they were opposed to more transparency for companies whose stock they'd be buying. "Time after time, we were met with surprise," says Kurt N. Schacht, head of the institute's Standards and Financial Market Integrity division. "They were mostly like 'What are you talking about? What letter?' So when we explained what we were calling about further, they'd say: 'Oh, that letter. Our trade association asked us to write it, so we did.' They had no idea what they were really writing about." The trade group that the treasurers were referring to was the American Bankers Association, the largest and most powerful lobbying outfit for the financial industry. So eventually FASB and its new chairman backed down on the valuation issue and the banks were allowed to do things as before.

Turn a Blind Eye to Weak Capital

Another type of regulatory forbearance has been very similar to Japan's experience in the 1990s, when the Asian nation's authorities delayed the full implementation of new capital rules that were agreed to internationally because their weak banks couldn't comply. That was the first set of Basel rules—named after the Swiss town where representatives from different countries gather to discuss them—that had targeted strengthening banks' capital base so they could withstand losses better. The second version came about in early 2000s, when global winds of deregulation tilted the balance in the banks' favor, in fact weakening the rules. Basel III was hammered out in 2009–2010, when the pendulum was swinging back, as the public blamed financial institutions for causing the worst economic crisis since World War II.[14] Even as the rules were tightened, the weak banks in Germany, France, the United States, and elsewhere lobbied heavily and succeeded to have their implementation postponed for another decade. While FDIC's Bair fought for faster enactment alongside Bank of England Governor Mervyn King and Swiss National Bank Chairman Philipp M. Hildebrand, other U.S. regulators weren't so keen on the rules taking effect too soon because of the difficulty weak U.S. banks would have with complying. Geithner, who frequently voiced support for tougher capital rules, didn't flex his muscles too much against the delay either. When Comptroller of the Currency John C. Dugan announced he'd be leaving in the middle of 2010 as the negotiations at the Basel Committee on Banking Supervision were getting heated, Geithner didn't make an effort to find a replacement who would strongly defend the United States side at the committee.

One of the ways Basel III is set to strengthen banks' capital base, so they can withstand future shocks without relying on government support and becoming zombies so easily, is through redefining what counts as basic regulatory capital. The 2008–2009 crisis showed that most of the stuff that was included in the consideration of capital were actually not able to absorb surging losses, so the definition was narrowed to common stock and several items taken out, such as mortgage servicing rights, which the U.S. banks rely on a lot. "The way you should think of capital is if you have losses, what will stop your creditors from running?" asks Anil Kashyap, a University of Chicago finance professor. "That's only equity capital, not all this other shaky stuff that has been included." If the new rules were to go into effect in 2011, Bank of America's capital ratio would halve to 4.5 percent, according to Keefe, Bruyette & Woods, an investment bank specializing in financial firms. Citigroup's would also be reduced by half to 5.4 percent (Figure 7.1). Basel III will require a common equity ratio of 7 percent under these new definitions, but not until 2019. Frederick Cannon, head of research at Keefe Bruyette, expects Citi and Bank of America to retain profits for many years to come so they can build their capital positions to comply with new Basel standards.

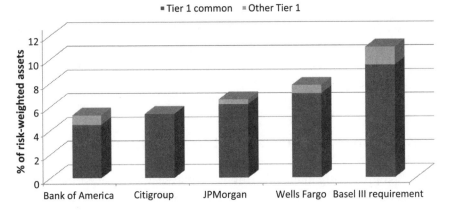

Figure 7.1 Capital ratios of the top U.S. banks calculated taking into account the changes to risk weightings and capital definitions, as if Basel III were in effect at the end of 2010 and based on banks' balance sheets at the time. Requirement figures include possible additional charges for the largest banks that were not finalized in 2011.

SOURCES: Keefe, Bruyette and Woods, Basel Committee on Banking Supervision, author's calculations.

In the discussion on an extra buffer for the largest global firms like Citi and Bank of America, Geithner again weighed in for softer requirements, siding with the Germans and the French. Another 1 to 2.5 percent capital may be added on for the biggest lenders, the Basel committee said in July 2011. Switzerland bumped up the minimum requirement for its two globally active banks to 19 percent in late 2010, without waiting for an agreement at Basel and going way beyond the international standards. The United States could follow suit if Geithner pushed for it. The financial regulatory overhaul passed by Congress in 2010 calls for tougher standards for the largest banks, without specifying what it needs to be. After Bair's departure in June 2011, there is no strong voice left to advocate a Swiss style buffer for the likes of Citi, insiders say. In new stress tests carried out in February–March 2011, the Federal Reserve used a 5 percent capital target for the 19 largest banks in the country and allowed most to resume paying dividends to shareholders, seeing them as well capitalized. Even so, Citi and Bank of America were left out from the group.[15] None of the big banks should have been allowed to start giving back capital to shareholders until they had built up healthy buffers as required under Basel III, according to Professor Kashyap. With the same reasoning, Bair urged patience before letting the banks return cash. Her advice was partly heeded, in the case of the weakest banks at least.

Bad Bank or Just an Administrative Concept?

Both Citigroup and Bank of America have set up so-called bad banks to separate their legacy assets and wind them down over time. But because there was no sale of the assets split off to another entity and the losses taken up front, these are not true bad banks similar to the Resolution Trust Corporation the government set up to clean up the savings and loans institutions in 1989. The Citi and Bank of America bad banks are mostly for presentation purposes, so that shareholders see a main unit that's making profit on its so-called core assets and the toxic stuff left from the crisis are in a special division that doesn't make the rest look as bad. Stiglitz calls this type of bad bank an "administrative concept," since it only changes the administrative reporting lines of departments. Citigroup called its bad bank Citi Holdings in January 2009 and shifted some $600 billion of mortgages, real estate, car loans, and securities into that unit, as well as some businesses it decided to divest from. It has managed to shrink Citi Holdings by 49 percent in two years, through sales, write-downs, and natural runoff as some loans mature.[16] The stuff that was easier to discard were probably sold first, and the remaining assets will be much harder to get rid of without big losses, estimates Joseph R. Mason, a former Treasury economist who's currently teaching finance at Louisiana State University. The bank's April 2011 operation to move some loans from one category to the other, in an effort to sell those, highlights such looming losses. Some estimate that the full cleanup could take a decade.[17] In July 2011, the bank was considering taking some of the businesses off the sale list, faced with difficulty in selling them and as pressure on it to shrink softened.[18]

Bank of America moved about $168 billion of trading assets and loans (mostly mortgages) into a bad bank in February 2011. In addition, about half of the $2.1 trillion of home loans the bank services for itself and others were shifted to the legacy asset division so it could be run down and also treated in a different manner. The legacy-asset cleanup will take time and more effort, analysts say.[19] Stiglitz believes a 1990s-style resolution corporation isn't necessary to set up a bad bank in the true sense. "What you really need to do is create new banks to hold the good assets and leave the bad assets with the old banks because the government doesn't really have an advantage in garbage disposal," he says. That's precisely how Iceland did it: Three new banks took over the good stuff and the creditors to the old banks were left with the proceeds from the eventual winding down of the rest. Citi and Bank of America are still holding onto the bad assets, not marking them down to sale prices, arguing it would still be a fire sale three years after the crisis, but they are able to fund them because the government's implicit and explicit backing has eased the availability of credit for the two institutions. "They know it's not a fire sale any more but they don't want to recognize the losses because they'd have to raise more capital to do so," says Stiglitz.

Tenuous Existence

While the banks take their sweet time to sell or run off toxic assets, downplay the losses they might incur while doing so, and face more losses from legal disputes, mortgage buybacks, and further deterioration in the housing market (more on the lurking losses in Chapter 9), the market doesn't believe them. The best indicator of the disbelief is the price-to-book ratio, which compares a company's market price to its book value, or what the management claims its equity is worth. When investors believe the management's valuation, this ratio is equal to or greater than 1. When they don't, it's below 1. Before the crisis, the average for U.S. and European banks was around 2, which meant investors were willing to pay a hefty premium for the franchise values of the banks beyond what their book value showed. In July 2011, the average price-to-book was 1.3 for the top 50 U.S. banks and 1.1 for the European banks. In the United States, Bank of America ranked lowest, with a 0.55 ratio, translating to investors believing that the

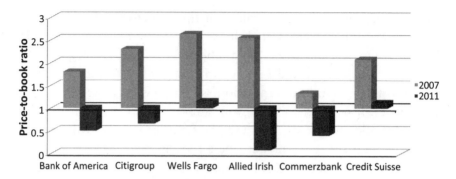

Figure 7.2 Weakening belief in banks' balance sheets showcased by the incredible drop in the price-to-book ratios of most banks in the United States and Europe. The ratio shows the relationship of the stock price to the value of the company's franchise indicated by management. A ratio of 1 indicates that the market values the firm the same as management; below 1 shows distrust in the value, and above 1 shows a premium awarded. While the zombies are well into the minus ratios, relatively healthier banks manage to cling onto positive ratios albeit much lower than four years ago.
SOURCE: Bloomberg Financial, LP.

value of the company is half of what its balance sheet shows. Citigroup ranked fourth from the bottom with 0.7, with two regional banks between them. In Europe, Allied Irish Bank was the bottom-feeder with 0.1, followed closely by Commerzbank with 0.42 (Figure 7.2).[20]

As the EU struggles with its sovereign debt crisis and the collapsing housing markets in several member states, the United States and its zombie banks might look like they're in better shape, but they actually aren't. With aggressive monetary easing by the Fed and tax breaks from the Treasury, the U.S. housing market postponed its full correction, while the economy and stock markets got temporary boosts. As the temporary relief wears off, there will be downward pressure on all fronts, exasperating losses for all the banks and endangering the zombies' livelihood once again. If the Fed starts raising interest rates, two-thirds of U.S. banks are vulnerable because they have more liabilities that would rise in cost than assets that would bring in higher returns. Several Bank of America subsidiaries rank among the most vulnerable, in a study of some 7,000 lenders.[21] While they struggle with losses and legacy assets that they can't get rid of for many years, the zombies short-change the economy because they can't fulfill their role of lending to companies and consumers. Bank of America abandoned McDonald's franchises around the country in 2008, refusing to extend them further credit as the bank struggled with its losses and acquisition of Merrill Lynch.[22] Although credit conditions have somewhat improved for the largest corporations, who can also access capital markets by selling bonds, small enterprises still struggle to get loans.[23] Government backing might keep weak banks on their feet, and they can slowly earn their way out, but meanwhile they hurt the economy. "When zombies win their gamble, the taxpayer doesn't get the windfall," says Boston College's Kane. "And meanwhile, new bubbles are being created with taxpayers' money and savers are being ripped off as interest rates are kept at zero. Until the losses are settled and balance sheets are cleaned up, zombie banks will be a drag."

Chapter 8

The Fight to
Rein in the Banks

I n January 2009, Barack Obama was inaugurated as the forty-
fourth president of the United States and handed a financial
calamity that almost everybody believed was caused by banks run
amok. In the same month, Paul A. Volcker first went public with his
idea to split banking from risky trading to put a safe distance between
the banks that the average American trusts to guard his money and
those gambling on everything from the weather patterns in Africa to
interest rates in Malaysia.

Although Volcker had been among Obama's circle of economic
advisors during the election campaign, his groundbreaking idea didn't
get much attention from the new president or his top economic
brass initially. In fact, Volcker struggled to start up a committee of
outside business and academic advisors that he was supposed to lead
because Timothy Geithner and Lawrence Summers—Obama's closest
advisors on economic matters—tried to keep the then-81-year-old
Volcker at a safe distance. But the man who tamed U.S. inflation in
the 1980s as the Chairman of the Federal Reserve wasn't one to give
up easily.

He complained about being kept out and got his group established in April. He led a small subgroup of his committee to meet with Obama in June, explaining the idea of the banking-trading separation. He met with more than a dozen senators who were willing to listen to it. Some of those senators were close to Vice President Joe Biden, who by that time was interested in Volcker's idea. In a White House meeting in December, in which different proposals for bank regulation were being debated, Biden told the group, which included Geithner and Summers: "I've been listening to this stuff for six months, but only Volcker makes sense." On Christmas Eve, when Volcker was heading to Virginia with his wife for the holidays, Summers—who had been opposed to the idea all along—asked him to stop by in Washington and talk about it more. Right after New Year's, Geithner's office called to inquire, too.[1] In January 2010, after a year of drumbeating, Volcker stood behind Obama with the smile of a tired warrior in a press conference during which the president presented Volcker's idea as a new addition to his administration's package of financial reforms and labeled it the Volcker Rule.

Like Volcker, a handful of other men and women have fought hard since the 2008 financial crisis to rein in the banks so they wouldn't continue taking the huge risks that brought down the global financial system. These fighters have met resistance from the banks' powerful lobbyists and their political allies. The rules they introduced got defeated or softened in lengthy battles. Their stories show the power of the financial sector and the difficulty in curbing that influence. But it's not all gloom and doom, either—the perseverance of these fighters have led to some achievements that will help the United States cope with future financial crises. The Volcker Rule, if enforced vigorously by regulators, could restrict the amount of gambling that banks do. The ability of the FDIC to seize failing bank-holding companies in addition to just banks (something Sheila Bair fought hard for) could make the largest firms more disciplined. The consumer protection agency, Elizabeth Warren's brainchild, may prevent banks or other financial institutions from being able to concoct enticing mortgage products that might then crash the market.

But more could have been done. Every crisis presents a pristine opportunity for policymakers to push through changes that would be hard to accomplish politically during normal times. Unfortunately that opportunity was squandered for the most part due to wrong priorities and bad advice.

Missed Opportunity

In early 2009, banks were vulnerable and politically weak to a degree that had been unseen for decades. Opinion polls showed widespread public anger toward them as the culprits of the worst economic downturn since the Great Depression.[2] The government had just rescued Citigroup and Bank of America, and even the strongest financial firms like Goldman Sachs had survived thanks to liquidity support from the Fed. Congressional leaders like Barney Frank and Christopher Dodd, who had consistently relied on campaign contributions from the financial industry and been their allies, were no longer willing to appear to be friends. Obama was elected on campaign rhetoric that bashed the banks and promised real change. After two decades of deregulation promoted and backed by Republican and Democratic administrations, the winds were strongly blowing against the sector. In the 1990s and 2000s, until the crash, consumer advocacy groups couldn't even get a vote to be held on any proposed reform that the banks opposed. But in 2009, the financial-services industry was already beginning to lose some battles. In May of that year, Congress overwhelmingly approved legislation that would restrict the fees they could charge on credit cards, a long-running sore spot for consumers.[3] Citi and Bank of America were still partially owned by the government and had to keep their voices down in Washington. Some of the largest trade associations that represent the banks' interests at the capital were divided and weak. All this represented a great opportunity to the new administration and the revamped Congress to establish a stronger regulatory regime that would reduce the likelihood of similar crises in the future. Unfortunately it went unused for the most part.

The relatively healthier banks were allowed to pay back their TARP funds in June 2009, the same month that the Treasury released its blueprint for new banking rules. JPMorgan Chase, Goldman Sachs, and other heavy hitters resumed their full-fledged lobbying activities just as Congressional leaders were getting ready to draft the legislation. In December, Citi and Bank of America were also allowed to pay back their government money and join the fray. Because Obama made health-care reform his priority, financial changes took the backseat and were delayed for months while Washington focused its energy on the former. And when it took the front stage finally, bickering among Democrats made it harder to push through strong regulations. Their lack of action also angered voters, who gave Republicans several election victories at the end of the year, including Scott Brown winning the late Ted Kennedy's senate seat in Massachusetts. All this gave the banks and their trade associations ample time to regroup, regain their strength, and fight vigorously against any attempt to restrain their risky activities. It also cost the Democrats their supermajority in the Senate, meaning they would need some Republican support to pass any law.

The electoral setback also jolted Obama to action, says Joseph Engelhard, a former U.S. Treasury deputy assistant secretary who is now a political analyst at Capital Alpha Partners. Volcker was seen by the public as the wise old man who wasn't afraid to stand up to Wall Street, so his idea had to be included in the reform package to regain credibility in the public's eyes, according to Engelhard. "Volcker was always sort of on the outside, and Geithner and Summers would have kept him there if it weren't for the election losses," Engelhard says. So Obama twisted the arms of his economic lieutenants to bring Volcker into the fold and made the January 2010 announcement about the Volcker Rule, even though both Frank's bill that had passed the House in December and Dodd's Senate version drawn up a month earlier had no mention of the separation of trading from banking. When Dodd only put in a vague section on the Volcker Rule in his revised set of rules in March, not laying out how it would be done, some senators spoke out and it became clear that Volcker wasn't fighting alone.

Volcker's Friends and Enemies

Senators Jeff Merkley of Oregon and Carl Levin of Michigan introduced an amendment to Dodd's bill that incorporated all of Volcker's ideas into legislative language.[4] The two senators then became the top generals in the fight to get the strongest Volcker Rule possible into law. Merkley was among the senators who met with Volcker in the summer of 2009, when the former Fed Chairman was making the rounds on Capitol Hill. The Oregon senator had seen the original proposal from Volcker and wanted to find out more. He was among the earliest converts. Levin got interested in the idea after executives of small companies from his state complained about the big banks and the lack of credit available. Community banks told Levin and his staff how Bank of America had stolen their clients in the boom years by offering cheaper loans and had now deserted those customers due to its financial difficulties. But the Michigan senator became a true convert while the Senate Investigations Subcommittee he chairs looked into Goldman's sale of toxic collateralized debt obligations (CDOs) to its clients, just as the housing market was showing cracks. During his committee's investigation and the hearings they culminated in, Levin saw the true face of the top financial institutions and wanted to curtail their bets against their customers with the knowledge they have as their brokers.

The Merkley-Levin amendment introduced in May wasn't only more detailed than the placeholder that Dodd had put into his bill in March, it was also much stricter than the initial language proposed by the Treasury to Congress. The Treasury's original text would leave much of the rule's tenets to be decided by the regulators and provided narrow definitions of proprietary trading—a bank using its own funds to make market bets. The senators' proposal laid out the details of how such bets would be restricted and how they'd be defined, with a much more encompassing range.[5] As the negotiations on the final shape of the Volcker Rule took place in May and June, Merkley and Levin coordinated with Volcker in twice-a-week conference calls. Michael S. Barr, who was the assistant secretary for financial institutions at the time, was the administration's point man on the discussions. Barr, whose academic passions lay with consumer protection, focused more on that part of the Dodd-Frank reform package and wasn't always there to back Merkley and Levin as the provisions of the Volcker Rule came under attack. At times, it felt like the two senators were fighting against the Treasury to keep the rules tight, instead of alongside it. The banks, which had lobbied Merkley and Levin early

on, gave up on them as too close to Volcker and took their concerns
to the Treasury, which then regularly voiced those in the debate. The
Treasury also wanted more say on the matter by the financial regulatory council that the new law was about to establish since it was going
to be chaired by the Treasury Secretary.

The Office of the Comptroller of the Currency (OCC), which
monitors national banks, wasn't always on Volcker's side either. There
were friendly OCC staff who'd go along with the senators' positions
only to be overturned by Julie L. Williams, the chief counsel of the
regulator since 1994. Williams had led the OCC's successful fight in
the early 2000s against state attorneys general who tried to go after
banks in their jurisdictions, arguing that federal banking law trumped
their powers.[6] The OCC didn't rein in the national banks nor did it
allow state regulators to do so, one of the reasons behind their unfet-
tered growth through unchecked activities. The Fed and the FDIC
weren't much involved in the Volcker Rule discussions, though the
FDIC was supportive and provided research help to the senators to
back their positions. Throughout Dodd-Frank negotiations, those
involved in the discussions say, Bair's FDIC was on one side of the
debate—tough rules to make sure risk was curtailed—and the OCC
was on the other, with the Fed in the middle. At the beginning, even
the Fed was on the opposition side, Bair says. But with the amount
of increased responsibility Dodd-Frank is giving the central bank, it
has come more toward the middle. The OCC naturally sees things
more from the banks' perspective because it has a closer tie as their
direct regulator, with examiners who reside in the financial institutions, Bair says. Others are more mincing with their words. "OCC
works like the banks' trading association," says Daniel Alpert, founder
of investment bank Westwood Capital and a financial restructuring
expert.

Fear of Lincoln's Amendment Helps Volcker

One development that helped Levin and Merkley in their fight to get
the Volcker Rule passed through Congress was a proposal by Blanche
Lincoln, a Democratic senator from Arkansas who headed the Senate

Agriculture Committee. Lincoln's amendment to the regulatory reform package suggested cordoning off units of banks that do any derivatives from the depository institutions.[7] That was seen as too far out there by Geithner, Dodd, and others trying to keep things in the center, who were frightened that it would drive away moderate Democrats and any Republican who'd back the financial reforms otherwise. The more that support for the Lincoln provision widened, the more mainstream the Volcker Rule looked in comparison. The Treasury called Volcker and his aides multiple times, asking him to speak out against the Lincoln approach. Finally Geithner himself called Volcker to make the request in person. The wise man agreed to do so, sending a letter to senators arguing that the Lincoln amendment's "extensive reach" wasn't necessary for sound regulation and that the Volcker Rule would do the trick.[8] In turn, his rule got more backing from Geithner, Dodd, and other Democratic leaders involved.

A final hurdle came from Scott Brown, the newly elected Massachusetts senator who'd become a key to the success of the reform bill clearing the chamber because Democrats needed four Republican votes to overcome a filibuster. One part of the Volcker Rule—prohibiting banks from owning hedge funds or private equity firms—would hurt State Street and Bank of New York Mellon, the former headquartered in Boston and the latter with significant presence there. So the lobbyists for those two firms camped in front of Brown's office for days, pressing him to get that section softened. These custodian banks, known as conservative institutions that don't take risk, were putting some of their clients' (such as pension funds) money into unregistered fund pools so they'd escape certain fees, and some of those had invested in subprime mortgages and blown up during the crisis. State Street ended up buying $2.5 billion of toxic assets from such funds it administered.[9] Because such investment vehicles counted as hedge funds and both firms had banking charters, they wanted the Volcker Rule's prohibition of banks owning hedge funds to be softened.

Dodd, who'd announced that he wasn't going to run for reelection, wanted to leave a legacy with some sort of reform enacted by Congress before he retired, and he needed Brown's vote for closure of debate in the senate. He weighed in with Merkley and Levin to cave in to Brown's demands. Obama wanted to have the U.S. reform in his pocket when he was going to meet other world leaders at the Group of 20 meetings coming up, so the administration pushed for a compromise too. One such compromise came when Volcker's hedge fund rule was watered down during negotiations that went into the wee hours of the night. The former Fed Chairman wasn't happy with what he was told the next morning, but he realized that was the best the political system was going to deliver at that conjuncture. Consequently, he issued a vague statement that praised the trading ban of the final version without mentioning the weakened hedge fund part.[10] Even after the weakening, the Volcker Rule is on top of U.S. banks' hate lists. In private conversations, public speeches, and reports, executives vent their frustrations about the regulation consistently. Whether it will live up to its expectations will depend on strict implementation by regulators. Meanwhile, Volcker has been sidelined, having been pushed out of his formal advisory role in January 2011.

The Republican Toughie

Although Republicans are generally thought of as advocates of deregulation and less government, the lines aren't so clear cut. While some Republicans have been proregulation, Democrats have been just as responsible in the two decades leading up to the 2008 crisis for dismantling rules that let banks run free. President Bill Clinton's Treasury Secretaries Robert Rubin and Lawrence Summers were as gung ho about unshackling the banks as their counterparts in both Bush administrations. Rubin (Geithner's mentor) and Summers (Obama's top economic advisor for the first two years of his presidency) put their signatures to two major efforts at deregulation, both directly responsible for the fomenting and enormity of the meltdown. They dismantled the Glass–Steagall Act of 1933, which had separated investment banking from commercial banking and provided relative financial stability for the next 70 years. They also prevented, with the help of former Fed Chairman Alan Greenspan (originally a Republican appointee), the regulation of derivatives, which then grew to a global market of $700 trillion.[11]

A lifelong Republican, there was very little hint of the proregulatory stance Bair would take as the head of the FDIC before her nomination by George W. Bush in 2006. Bair had worked for Republican Senate Majority Leader Robert Dole for eight years and served as Assistant Treasury Secretary in Bush's first term. Perhaps the only clue might have come from her membership on the board of the Center for Responsible Lending, a nonpartisan group that has advocated better regulations for mortgages and other bank loans. Still, Bair's candidacy sailed through, unlike the top choice for the job, Diana Taylor, whose antigun views drew the wrath of the National Rifle Association and led Bush to drop her before going public with her nomination.[12] Bair shone as the most sensible regulator during the last few months of Bush's presidency, fighting for the rights of the taxpayer during the height of the crisis as Treasury Secretary Henry Paulson, Fed Chairman Ben Bernanke, and NY Fed President Timothy Geithner rushed to save the big banks at any cost. Bair also outshone most of her Democratic colleagues in Obama's first three years pushing for the toughest regulations to reduce future risks of the banks and lessen the bill for the government. "There were interesting issues that attracted me to the position, but those were not the ones that I ended up dealing with," she says. "I thought it was going to be a 9-to-5 kind of job."

Bair fought Geithner on the rescue of Citigroup to make sure unnecessary subsidies weren't provided and that shareholders paid for the mistakes. She also pushed for a management change but didn't get to win that one. "Geithner hates Bair because she was doing her job, and Geithner was trying to subsidize the banks," says Joseph Stiglitz, a former advisor to Clinton and Nobel laureate in economics. Another proregulation Republican, Senator Susan Collins of Maine, approached Bair as Dodd-Frank was being formulated. Collins, who had started her public career as a financial regulator in her state, felt that something had to be done with the capital of the biggest banks to make them safer. She asked Bair whether they could formulate something together. So they came up with the Collins Amendment, which put a floor on how much capital bank holding companies need to hold and eliminated the use of some hybrid bonds as capital. Collins was among the four Republicans who voted for Dodd-Frank at the end.

Bair thought even Glass–Steagall could be revived, but she was disappointed to see very little support for that idea. Another Republican, Senator John McCain, was a co-sponsor of a bill that would bring Glass–Steagall back. It didn't garner much support when McCain, Obama's rival in the 2008 presidential elections, didn't put his weight behind it. Bair successfully fought for a resolution authority that could wind down the holding companies. The FDIC previously had authority only to seize and liquidate the depository banks, which are only one part of the giant financial conglomerates. She didn't get her wish to have an additional fund to pay for such a resolution that would be collected from the largest banks in advance (more on the merits of these rules in Chapter 11). Because of her tough stance, "the big banks hate Bair," says Edward Kane, professor of economics at Boston College.

In addition to her advocacy at home, Bair was the leading pro-regulatory voice representing the United States internationally. The Basel Committee on Banking Supervision, which sets capital standards for banks worldwide, debated stronger standards in 2009–2010. She championed and won a global leverage standard, a simple capital-to-assets ratio that ignores the sophisticated and easily gamed risk-weighting of assets so as to put a hard cap on the borrowing of banks. This idea was ridiculed when she first floated it internationally in 2006. She was called a Luddite by some of her critics at the time because risk management had advanced so much that a simple consideration of total assets without paying attention to their risk looked way out of date. Of course, Bair was proven right when the banks blew up. All their claims of having mastered risk management so well evaporated when those risks brought them down. And, their capital levels were incredibly low to cope with the losses thanks to Basel rules allowing smaller reserves in the 2000s with the help of the risk-weighting magic. The European banks leveraged themselves up to the tilt before the crisis because they had no simple leverage ratio. The U.S. banks already had such a ratio domestically implemented, so they shifted the toxic assets to German *landesbanks* or hid them in off-balance-sheet entities. The new Basel leverage standard agreed in 2010 includes off-balance-sheet assets in the calculation of the total, in order to close that loophole.[13]

Germany, France, and some other countries worried that their banks could not comply with the tougher rules. In exchange for getting tougher rules accepted, Bair and her proregulation allies on the Basel committee compromised on the timing of their implementation. So the definition of capital was narrowed, a new leverage ratio was brought in, the minimum capital ratios were increased, the calculation of risk was streamlined to crack down on manipulation, but the implementation of all these were spread out to a decade or more. And since everything was finalized in December 2010, cracks have already appeared in implementation in Europe and the United States. The Europeans are balking at enforcing the leverage ratio and other provisions of Basel III.[14] U.S. regulators dragged their feet in writing Basel changes into the rulebook, hoping that they could soften them after Bair's departure in mid-2011. There were no signs of progress two months after she left either.

Finding Ways to Skinny the Banks

Alongside Bair's resolution authority and the Volcker Rule, there were other attempts to enact legislation to clamp down on the financial sector's risks. Senators Sherrod Brown and Ted Kaufman, Democrats from Ohio and Delaware, respectively, were consistent backers of stronger banking rules. They supported Levin and Merkley in their fight. Yet they wanted to do more, especially to rein in the biggest U.S. banks, which had become too big to fail and were rescued with taxpayer money during the crisis (Figure 8.1). So in April 2010, they introduced the Safe Banking Act to put concrete limits on the size of the nation's lenders. The proposed law targeted the nondeposit liabilities of banks and put a cap on them (each couldn't exceed 2 percent of the nation's GDP).[15] That would force the six largest banks—Bank of America, JPMorgan Chase, Citigroup, Wells Fargo, Goldman Sachs, and Morgan Stanley—to break up. Wells Fargo, which is mostly deposit-focused, would be the least impacted and could get away with a 1 to 2 percent contraction, whereas the other five would have to shed 30 to 50 percent of their assets or divide themselves in two to comply with the act. Their legislation would complement the Volcker

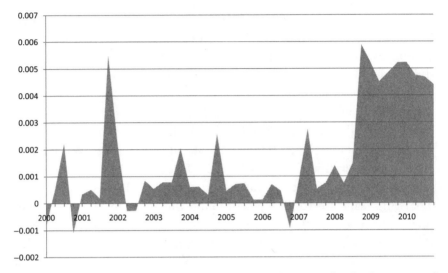

Figure 8.1 Bigger Borrows Cheaper. The gap between the funding costs of banks with assets more than $100 billion and those with assets between $10 billion and $100 billion.

SOURCE: İnci Ötker-Robe, Aditya Narain, Anna Ilyina, Jay Surti, "The Too-Important-to-Fail Conundrum: Impossible to Ignore and Difficult to Resolve." International Monetary Fund, Monetary and Capital Markets Department report, May 27, 2011. Based on FDIC data and IMF staff computations.

Rule, Kaufman says. "All of these are ways to skinny the banks so they aren't too big to fail," says the former Biden aide who filled his senate seat when Biden became vice president.

The proposal came under attack from the banks immediately and the Treasury, of course. JPMorgan, which had usurped Bank One in 2004 and still has about 10,000 employees based in Columbus—a remnant of Bank One's operations there—warned Brown that his state would lose thousands of jobs if JPMorgan was forced to get smaller. Brown wouldn't budge with that threat because he actually had seen how the merger of Bank One with JPMorgan led to 6,000 job cuts at the time. A Treasury memo to Brown's office on a Saturday listed eight reasons why the department was opposed to the proposed legislation. Those reasons were mostly centered on the traditional argument made by banks all the time that risk needs to be taken into account when measuring size—the tenet that Basel II was based on and which was proved wrong during the crisis.

Despite Senate Majority Leader Harry Reid's support, the Safe Banking Act didn't make it too far. Republicans opposed it as a block even though Brown and Kaufman were hoping for some support from rural states where small banks and small companies are hurt by the largest banks. Because Dodd didn't back the proposal, the Democratic members of the banking committee also went against it. "Dodd wanted a bill and this was too big a risk for him," Kaufman says. So the act mustered only 33 votes in the Senate and died.

The Farm Boy versus Goliath

Thomas M. Hoenig was born and raised in a small Iowa town in the middle of farm country, went to college in Kansas, and straight out of school joined the regional Federal Reserve bank in Missouri, which covers all those states and a bit more farmland in neighboring states. He has spent his life dealing with farmers, small companies, and community banks, but he also had first-hand experience of too-big-to-fail (TBTF) financial institutions. When Oklahoma City-based lender Penn Square Bank ran into trouble in 1982, he was in charge of bank supervision and told his bosses that the bank wasn't viable and the Kansas City Fed shouldn't give it emergency loans. His response to Penn Square's president asking for funds, which he calls the "sorry-Charlie-we're-not-going-to-lend" letter, is framed in the ground-floor museum of the central bank. But Penn Square's failure had far-reaching consequences, contributing to the collapse two years later of Continental Illinois Bank, considered to be the first TBTF case in U.S. financial history. Although Continental Illinois was rescued by the Fed, at least its shareholders were wiped out and taxpayers got the proceeds from its recovery, Hoenig says three decades later. "That was much better than the rescues this time around," adds Hoenig.

Soon after becoming the Kansas City Fed's president in 1991, Hoenig started to speak against TBTF banks and the dangers they pose for the financial system. He raised the issue in Fed meetings in Washington when Greenspan was the chairman. "There was silence on the other side of the table," recalls Hoenig of the former Fed Chairman's approach to any demand for more regulation. "It wasn't only Greenspan's philosophy, but also that of Congress, administration, regulators too. The momentum was to deregulate." He spoke against Basel II relaxing capital requirement for banks, bringing it up with Greenspan's successor Bernanke. The new chairman seemed to listen more, but he didn't move to do anything differently either. After the 2008 crisis, Hoenig pressed Bernanke and the other Fed governors in Washington to support more stringent regulation on the biggest banks, to no avail. He sent them a detailed proposal on how TBTF banks should be resolved in the future. Nobody was interested. "Rescuing bad banks isn't capitalism; it's corporate socialism," he says.

Starting in early 2010, Hoenig also loudly opposed the Fed keeping its zero percent interest rate to help the wounded banks repair their balance sheets. While they're being rescued with a backdoor subsidy, the policy is creating new bubbles worldwide, he argued: commodity prices surging, agricultural land prices going up in the United States, housing prices rising in China, and more. "It's just a matter of time before another crisis comes to pop the current bubble we're pushing," Hoenig says. Even though he's been a tireless warrior, Hoenig is on his way out, just like Bair, Volcker, and Kaufman. Hoenig will be retiring in October 2011 after four decades at the Kansas City Fed.

Never-Ending Assault

As some of the key combatants for stronger bank regulation depart, the rules that aim to rein in the financial sector are under continuing attack with even more vigor, as the banks have rebuilt their lobbying coffers with Fed's covert subsidy. Volcker is worried that the regulators won't interpret the prop trading rules as broadly as he and Congress intended. Bair is concerned regulators won't use the resolution powers over financial conglomerates when the next crisis hits. Kaufman is anguished that the biggest banks have gotten bigger since 2008. While the regulators around the world debate implementing tougher rules, the banks play the governments against each other, making the age-old argument that if there's too much regulatory burden in one place, they'll move to another country with more lax

Table 8.1 What Made It and What Didn't

The Good Stuff That Passed	The Good Stuff That Failed	In Limbo
Volcker Rule: Hedge fund section watered down; implementation depends on regulators	**Safe Banking Act:** Would have split up the largest U.S. banks	**Basel III leverage and liquidity:** Agreed to in 2010 but might not be implemented fully or globally at the end
Resolution Authority: Cross-border resolution mechanism still missing; many are doubtful that politicians will use the authority	**Return of Glass-Steagall:** Would have separated investment and commercial banking	
Basel III Capital: Some parts watered down; implementation delayed for a decade		

laws. The European banks threaten to move to New York while the U.S. banks threaten to move to Europe.

Instead of holding the line and acting together to crack down on the industry, the governments on both sides of the Atlantic buy into these threats and weaken their planned rules consistently (Table 8.1). Two weeks after Barclays and HSBC—both London-based banks—issued veiled warnings that they might move shop, a British commission softened its proposal for new rules, dropping its demand for investment and commercial banking to split, à la Glass-Steagall.[16] Hoping the public's memory of the crisis is fading away, even the apologies made during the crisis are being reversed. Greenspan, who had pretty much said *mea culpa* for his lack of regulation and keeping interest rates too low for too long, began to publicly lobby against the implementation of Dodd-Frank reform package in early 2011.[17] "Dodd-Frank is being lobbied down in the rule-making process since different regulators have to do that and they're not all like the FDIC," says Boston College's Kane. As finance has gotten more and more complicated, the sector has also had an easier monopoly on information. "Since the banks are the gurus on financial everything, politicians believe them when they say it'll be the end of the world if they fail," says Stiglitz.

Some of the fighters against that monopoly remain in the trenches. Elizabeth Warren, a law professor at Harvard University who has written books about the consumers' plight, is shaping the new Consumer Financial Protection Bureau despite Geithner's dislike of her. In mid-2011, Warren was playing a key role in the negotiations between state attorneys general and the big banks to straighten out their mortgage servicing practices. In September, she announced her candidacy for a Senate seat in Massachusetts to challenge Scott Brown. Senators Merkley and Levin plow on, introducing new legislation to hold the banks accountable, urging prosecutors to look into their abuse of clients, pressing the regulators to implement the financial reforms thoroughly.[18] Bair, on her way out of the FDIC, appointed Volcker to a committee that will advise the bank regulator on how to wind down the biggest banks when they collapse.[19] Volcker also continues to be the voice of wisdom, making public comments to hold the regulators' and the politicians' feet to the fire.

Chapter 9

To Foreclose or Not to Foreclose?

David Blanchflower, an economics professor at Dartmouth College, spends a lot of time in southern Florida, where the most spectacular housing bubble has given way to the worst bust in the United States. Blanchflower tells the story of a Florida limo driver to illustrate the problems still facing the nation's housing market. The driver bought his house for $300,000 at the peak of the market, putting $100,000 down and borrowing the rest. In early 2011, a house similar to his down the street sold for $82,000. The driver was continuing to pay his mortgage, but questioning why he should keep doing so. "I make these payments so the bankers can pay themselves all these bonuses," he told Blanchflower. "My mortgage is in good shape, but why don't I just walk?" The driver's case points to the inherent problem of underwater mortgages and the decreasing incentive homeowners have to continue paying, the professor says. In addition, the mortgage is probably valued at $200,000 on the bank's books, when it's really worth $80,000, which highlights the losses that are lurking in the shadows but are unlikely to be avoided forever, Blanchflower says.

Matthew Weidner is an attorney who fights foreclosures in central Florida, where the home price declines haven't been as severe as the southern part of the state. Weidner talks about his clients' failed efforts to negotiate with their banks for a mortgage modification. "The bank doesn't know who really owns the mortgage, so they can't modify it," Weidner says. Foreclosures dropped in early 2010 in the area because of the irregularities discovered nationwide with the process, but there's no real permanent solution in the horizon, Weidner says.

The issues Blanchflower and Weidner point to in Florida are shared by the wider U.S. housing market. Those and many more unresolved problems have prevented the market from fully correcting so it can rebound. On the one hand, government efforts to make it less painful for homeowners, and on the other, weak banks' inability to shoulder all the losses that a bottoming out would entail, have prolonged prices from reaching bottom. Home foreclosures may have remained lower than expected, but that hasn't been due to a fundamental recovery. Instead, it has been because of the legal and financial troubles banks face, as well as government efforts to slow them. That might have eased the pain for homeowners, but it has also held back the nation's economic recovery, adding to the woes caused by the lack of credit from zombie banks. The lingering problems of the U.S. housing market are similar to Europe's sovereign blues: Because of weak banks, the necessary restructuring of debt cannot be done. Foreclosing on defaulted mortgages is very costly for the nation and the banks themselves. On the other hand, sharing the pain of a collapsed housing market between the borrowers and the lenders through principal reductions—as undertaken in Iceland—could clear the market faster. But just as the European Union (EU) refuses to make its banks share the pain, so too does the United States.

Protecting Home Equity Loans

During the housing boom in the United States—when prices more than doubled in a decade—borrowing against the equity of the house to spend on other things became popular. Because the price of the house was constantly increasing, even if the homeowner had made only interest payments for the first several years, he could cash in the price increase by refinancing the mortgage and buy a new car with the difference. Of course, this wasn't true equity built through payments, but just a windfall of rising markets. The banks loaned more than $1 trillion this way. The biggest four banks still have about $420 billion of such loans on their books, led by Bank of America with some $140 billion.[1] The big four are also the largest servicers of mortgages in the country, with about 55 percent of the market. Again Bank of America leads the pack, collecting payments for $2 trillion in home loans nationwide (Figure 9.1).[2] The home equity loans have performed much better than mortgages overall. Homeowners who default on their mortgages continue to pay their home equity loans since they need the credit line open from the bank, and many probably think the bank can come after other assets if they default on their loan (unlike the nonrecourse mortgage), according to Laurie Goodman, senior managing director at Amherst Securities and one of the best known analysts in the field. The borrowers may also value the relationship with their bank, which gave them the home equity loan, whereas the mortgage may be from a broker or other source, says Fitch Ratings analyst Christopher Wolfe.

In most states, there's no recourse in either case other than the collateral, which is the house. And the mortgage has priority claim over the home equity loan (referred to as first and second liens on the property). So, in case of a foreclosure, the lender of the mortgage collects whatever the house sells for minus legal costs and, if anything is left, then the second lien is paid. When the house is underwater, as is the case with about a quarter of mortgages nationwide, and the built-up equity isn't enough to cover the gap, then the likelihood drops to zero for the bank holding the second lien getting any money.

That has created perverse incentives for the top banks. They've resisted modifying the mortgages they service because that could threaten the performance of their home equity loans. So as part of their pretend-and-extend strategy, the banks keep the second liens on their books at full value (since they're still performing) even though they will have no real value once the house is foreclosed because the first lien is in default and it will have priority over the second lien in recovery. Thus, the largest banks have hampered government efforts

Mortgage servicing

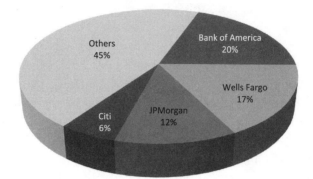

Second liens and revolving credit

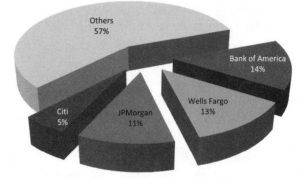

Figure 9.1 The nation's top four banks service more than half the mortgages and own almost half the second-lien loans.

SOURCES: Amherst Securities based on data from Inside Mortgage Finance, Federal Reserve, and FDIC.

to modify loans to make them more affordable, but that has only prolonged the day of reckoning and could end up costing more through massive losses of their second-lien portfolios, which add up to about 80 percent of the four top banks' capital.[3] Former Senator Ted Kaufman, who headed the Congressional Oversight Panel looking at the government efforts to prevent foreclosures, says the servicers have another conflict of interest in the modification equation. They get more fees from making a foreclosure than they would get from a modification, Kaufman says. Of course, in the end, a foreclosure would hurt the servicer banks' interests more by destroying the value of their second liens. So the big question is: To foreclose or not to foreclose? That question lies at the heart of the solution to the housing rut in the country.

Banks Wave the Moral-Hazard Card

When Treasury Secretary Timothy Geithner was asked during a Congressional hearing why the government hasn't backed principal reductions on outstanding home loans as a way to prevent foreclosures, he responded by saying that it would be wrong to spend "taxpayers' money so that people can afford to stay in a home that's really beyond their capacity to afford."[4] That has been the bedrock of the banks' arguments against forgiving principal for mortgages that are underwater. Millions of consumers who bought houses they couldn't afford share the blame for the financial crisis, banks say. Pardoning their debt partially would lead to moral hazard, which is the classic argument that a decision maker will repeat the same risks in the future if he doesn't face the consequences of his soured bet. If homeowners get mortgage relief now, they will take on mortgages they can't afford in the future, with the understanding they'll be rescued again. It will also lead to many who can afford to keep on paying also walking away in order to get a principal reduction, the banks say. The banks and their executives easily forget that the biggest moral hazard has been created by the trillions of dollars spent to rescue the banks during the 2008 crisis, with the zombies remaining intact, their creditors spared any pain. Banks, knowing that the government will come to their rescue, will keep on (and are already) taking the same big risks that led to their collapse. The biggest beneficiaries of moral hazard have the audacity to oppose it when millions of homeowners who have lost their jobs or seen their house prices reduced by half struggle to pay.

Geithner, the banks' best friend, ignores the fact that most homeowners *can* afford the homes at the prices that they've come down to but are forced to pay back a loan at the original price. Clearly, both the borrowers and the lenders took a bet that real estate prices would keep rising. But somehow Geithner and his banker allies want to punish only the borrowers for their soured investment, not the lenders who were part of the original wager. That's very similar to the EU's denial that Ireland or Greece's mistakes of overspending were made possible by the German and French banks that lent them the money to do so.

Principal Reduction: The Bogeyman

Amherst's Goodman thinks the only solution to the U.S. housing crisis is forcing the banks to forgive some of the principal on mortgages. In coordination with that partial reduction, the second liens must be substantially eliminated, she argues. Goodman counters Geithner's and the banks' moral-hazard argument by pointing out that this has to be thought of as an economic issue, not a moral one. Preventing fore-closures artificially won't solve the problem, she says. "We're just stretching it to the future," Goodman warns.

The International Monetary Fund (IMF) agrees, saying that more value is destroyed through foreclosures, and that the recoveries from the loan drop as the process stretches. A 15 percent principal reduc-tion on first and second liens would cost the top 40 U.S. banks about $350 billion, the IMF calculated in April 2011. Yet the Fund acknowl-edged that mortgage servicers didn't favor such reductions because their fees from servicing would decline. Its exercise was also very generous on the second liens, which is where the biggest banks would hurt most. Another major hurdle to principal reductions in the United States is securitization. The IMF calculations were only based on the $2.1 trillion of home loans held on banks' balance sheets. Another $7.1 trillion are in mortgage-backed securities.[5] Because the owners of these bonds are dispersed worldwide, and each pool holds thousands of individual loans, it's much harder to agree to a principal reduction for a single homeowner. In other words, there's a serious disconnect between the borrower and the lender for the vast majority of U.S. mortgages outstanding.

Most of those securitized loans are also serviced by the big four banks, which also don't favor principal reductions. "The biggest problem is borrowers can't talk to their lenders," says former Senator Kaufman. "So how could they even negotiate a modification, let alone a principal reduction?" Securitizations have also slowed down foreclosures because it is unclear who the owners of the loans are, the original promissory notes are missing, and on and on. Though more painful and costly, foreclosures would eventually clear the housing market. "The servicers don't know who owns the mortgages," says Florida lawyer Weidner. That bogs down the legal process, he says. The courts in his state and elsewhere are overwhelmed with millions of foreclosure cases with missing documents, mostly due to securitizations, Weidner adds. A foreclosure on average takes about twice as long now compared to the precrisis era. Sales of foreclosed homes have also slowed by about 50 percent, making the clearing of the market even more difficult (Figure 9.2).[6]

The irregularities in the foreclosures led to a nationwide investigation by state attorneys general in early 2011. Some prosecutors found that banks were processing foreclosure documents without the proper documentation and assigning robo-signers to authorize them without any study of the borrower's situation. In the negotiations that ensued between the attorneys general and the top servicer banks, the principal-reduction option was floated by Elizabeth Warren, the brains behind the Consumer Financial Protection Bureau (CFPB) and the banks' nemesis. Yet it was quickly quashed by attorneys general sympathetic to the lenders and Warren's efforts to negotiate a financial deal were undermined by the Federal Reserve that cut a softer deal quickly. A $20 billion settlement requested by Warren was also reduced to $5 billion.[7] R. Christopher Whalen, who runs a research firm rating U.S. banks, says the banks cannot restructure mortgages through principal reduction because they lack the capital to meet the losses that would incur.

Servicing Costs Rise

Part of the mess is due to the lack of personnel the banks have committed to mortgage servicing. When the crisis started and losses stacked up, banks culled their employees to reduce costs. Close to 200,000 were let go in the United States alone, led by—you guessed it—Bank of America and Citigroup, which have both cut over 40,000 jobs each.[8] These cuts came at a time when servicing would require more manpower as delinquencies, defaults, and foreclosures all surged. No wonder the banks had to assign robo-signers to process documents. They just don't have the resources. JPMorgan, the least harmed from

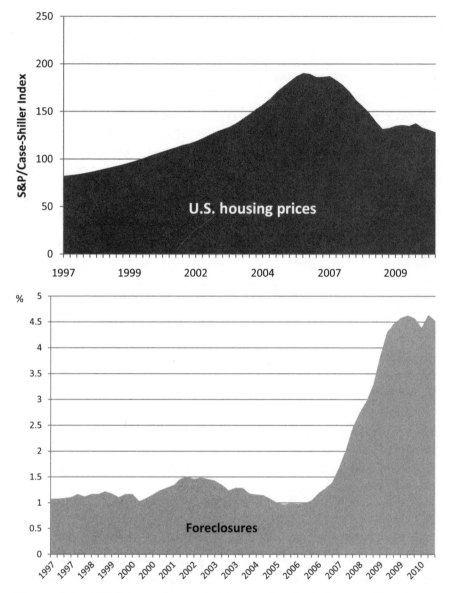

Figure 9.2 U.S. house prices tripled in two decades before tumbling down. Foreclosures have surged since the breakout of the crisis, but probably not enough to clear the system.

Both data as of 2011 first quarter.

SOURCES: Standard & Poor's, Mortgage Bankers Association.

the crisis, said in April 2011 that it would hire 3,000 people to work on troubled mortgages. Bank of America, which services about twice as many loans as JPMorgan, said it has hired 2,700 in the first quarter to do so. Citigroup is adding 500 employees to the loan-modification division.[9] Rising servicing costs will eat into the profits of the banks, and the zombie banks will be restrained by their weak profitability to commit the necessary resources. "We can either protect the banks or fix the housing market," says Damon Silvers, who was the deputy chairman of the Congressional Oversight Panel.[10] "The whole housing finance system is structured around unrealistic values, and that's strangling consumer demand, and consequently the larger economy. Foreclosures need to stop because they are the most destructive possible way of managing a deflating housing bubble and tend to produce a downward spiral. If regulators and auditors insisted on honesty about the value both of housing and of home mortgages, bank forbearance would collapse." Silvers argues that the banks have to reduce principal on mortgages because the original loans are based on inflated values of houses that have since come down.

Either way the banks will have to record further losses before the housing market and the economy can recover completely. If they're forced to forgive some principal, then it will be more upfront and the zombies' fallibility will be revealed. If they're allowed to continue with pretend-and-extend by slowly going through foreclosures, the pain will be spread to a longer time period, but that will also mean the recovery will take longer, similar to Japan's lost decade of the 1990s. In the second option, 11 million people could lose their homes, Amherst's Goodman predicts. That would be one in every five homeowners, in addition to the 5 million foreclosures already completed in 2008–2010. Those would bring down home prices more, reduce the recoveries from the foreclosed assets, and cut into consumers' purchasing power further. After falling by 31 percent, prices recovered slightly in 2009, thanks to the government's tax breaks for new homeowners and loan modification efforts. Those were both temporary fixes. The modifications have resulted in delinquencies again because they didn't involve principal reductions. The tax credit expired, so prices entered a new decline phase in the second quarter of 2010 and the national average has gone down by 7 percent since. Robert Shiller, whose Case-Shiller index is among the most trusted housing price gauges, sees another 25 percent decline possible.[11]

The banks also lack the resources to sell the houses on which they foreclose, which has slowed down that process as well. The big four banks had about $10 billion of foreclosed property at the end of March 2011.[12] The current backlog of foreclosed properties in the U.S. banking system, almost 1 million homes, would take about four years to clear, analysts estimate.[13] Another 5–10 million would mean at least a decade before those houses are sold, all the while bringing prices further down. Meanwhile, the slower foreclosure process has allowed millions of people to stay in their homes without paying rent or the mortgage for extended periods. The so-called squatter's rent is estimated to be $50 billion in 2011, according to JPMorgan Chase. That's clearly value the banks are losing from their properties.

Crappy Mortgages Returned

Although three-quarters of outstanding residential mortgages in the United States aren't held on bank balance sheets, that doesn't mean they can't come back to haunt the banks that originated them or packaged them into the mortgage-backed securities (MBS). Freddie Mac and Fannie Mae, the two government-controlled mortgage giants, which were the top clients for the MBS, have been asking banks to buy back loans that they're now discovering weren't underwritten properly. Freddie and Fannie have managed to get some $21 billion back from such mortgages since 2008, according to the Financial Crisis Inquiry Commission. The two government agencies struck deals with the biggest banks that got them off the hook for more put-backs, another back-door subsidy provided to the sector. But private investors who bought the MBS from the banks before the crisis are demanding buybacks as well. Bank of America faces such demands from a group of bondholders, including the nation's largest bond managers who hold $84 billion of securities. The bank's exposure to buyback demands could reach $222 billion. About $400 billion of MBS sold to private investors by the four biggest banks are at risk of being returned.[14] The losses to the banks from such put-backs could reach $100 billion, Amherst's Goodman estimates. Such bad underwriting isn't only limited to precrisis loans either. Similar flaws were found in 15 percent of loans Citigroup sold to Freddie Mac in late 2009 to early 2010, according to a *Bloomberg News* analysis.[15] The insurers of MBS are also starting to demand such reimbursements now that they've managed to stay alive, says Fitch's Wolfe. The put-backs from the insurers come back with a big delay also because they happen only after a loan is liquidated, according to Amherst's Goodman. Therefore, such demands could be coming for another five years, she says.

Bank of America has tried to reach agreements with such claimants, getting another sweet deal from the government through Freddie and Fannie settlements that allowed the bank to pay a pittance for the losses the mortgage-financing giants have been facing due to such crappy loans sold by the bank. In June 2011, it also reached an $8.5 billion deal with some private mortgage-bond owners. The settlement, which would allow the bank to pay only 9 percent of the losses the bonds face, was challenged in court by other bondholders. Even if it mustered court approval, the deal would cover about half the bank's exposure to such claims.[16]

The defaults of mortgages inside the MBS reflect the real problems that are lurking on the banks' own balance sheets, argues Daniel Alpert, founder of investment bank Westwood Capital and a financial restructuring expert. Although the banks argue that their portfolios are better than what is inside the MBS, the loans packaged into the bonds and those on the banks' books should be similar, Alpert says. So the delinquency and default rates reported by the banks—declining since 2010—are overly optimistic, and the banks pretend a bigger chunk of their home loans are performing than they really are, according to Alpert. "When the bank gets one payment in the 120-day period where the loan would be marked delinquent, the clock is reset," he says. Taking the prepayment, default, and liquidation data of the MBS universe as his basis, Alpert has calculated that the nonperforming bank loans should total about $704 billion, and $275 billion of that would be on the biggest four lenders' balance sheets. That's more than twice the amount currently presented as nonperforming by the big four. A similar underreporting is occurring in commercial real estate loans—for malls, hotels, office buildings, and the like, according to Fitch Ratings.[17]

When the Levees Are Opened

The efforts to prop up the housing market since 2008 through tax credits, by driving down interest rates, and by other means may have succeeded in delaying the day of reckoning for the banks, but it can't be put off forever. Almost all new mortgages issued since the crisis have been backed by some federal entity because the banks cannot take on any more home loans before fixing the legacy problems, which could take years. Meanwhile, Congress is discussing the end to Fannie and Freddie's role in mortgages. The government cannot extricate itself from housing finance because it hasn't forced the banks to clean up shop. If the two mortgage giants retreated from the scene, the housing market would collapse even further. The Federal Reserve's quantitative easing through the purchase of $2 trillion of securities including MBS has also kept interest rates low, making homes more affordable and prevented prices from tumbling more. With the end of such policies in 2011, rates are likely to rise and hurt home afford-ability, and thus prices. "The housing market hasn't cleared because of government backing, or prices would have collapsed," says Frederick Cannon, head of research at Keefe, Bruyette & Woods, an investment bank specializing in financial firms.

The Fed has tried to get some inflation so asset values can go back up and the losses lurking on the banks' balance sheets don't have to be recognized, says James G. Rickards, an advisor to fund managers. However, it's not working because the money is flowing to emerging markets to create inflation there and not helping to do the same in the United States. Even a third round of quantitative easing, if attempted, won't really help because the banks' balance sheets aren't fixed and companies are afraid to spend their cash before the funda-mental problems are tackled, says Desmond Lachman at the American Enterprise Institute. So once again, the denial over zombie banks' troubles can hold back a nation's recovery for many years, as it did in Japan in the 1990s. The lessons, it seems, are never learned.

Chapter 10

Bigger Banks, More Derivatives, Higher Risk

I n September 2010, some of Ireland's government guarantees for bank debts were about to expire, which put U.S. Treasury officials on edge. If the guarantee wasn't renewed, the banks would likely default on their bonds, triggering the next event in line: a slew of credit default swap (CDS) contracts on the banks' debt. U.S. Treasury officials had reason to worry—the names backing those contracts were the largest U.S. banks, and they could end up paying billions in case of default. Any more weight on U.S. banks could be a tipping point to collapse. Treasury officials made inquiries to their counterparts at the Irish finance ministry, asking about the course of action the country was planning to take and indicated their concern about possible default and its CDS repercussions. A year after having issued blanket guarantees on the banks' liabilities, the Irish government once again didn't dare let the banks fail. Instead it ended up asking for financial assistance from the European Union (EU) and the International Monetary Fund (IMF); the country had been pushed to the brink of collapse.

CDS and other derivatives, financial contracts that are based on the prices of stocks, bonds, commodities, and other assets or securities, exacerbated the 2008 crisis because the losses from the U.S. housing market woes were multiplied by bets on that market. Derivatives started out as useful instruments to shift risk: A farmer can lock in the price of corn before harvest so he doesn't have to worry about declining prices by then, and a carmaker exporting most of its output can make sure it doesn't get burned by swings in exchange rates. Yet the explosion in the derivatives market in the last decade, especially the contracts that are traded over the counter (OTC derivatives) and not on exchanges, wasn't the result of this kind of use, but financial-market players betting on everything from weather patterns to platinum prices. The OTC market grew eightfold in a decade, peaking at $673 trillion in mid-2008 (Figure 10.1). During that same time frame, the world's economic output only doubled to $61 trillion, and the market value of companies listed on stock exchanges grew by a paltry one-third to $45 trillion. Nonfinancial users of the contracts account for less than 10 percent of the total market.[1] The bottom line is that derivatives aren't serving the economy's needs: They've been turning the financial system to a great big casino. The growth in OTC

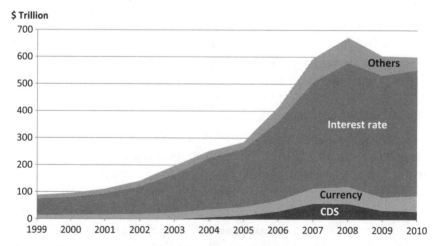

Figure 10.1 Explosion of Derivatives 1999–2010. Over-the-counter derivatives outstanding worldwide.

SOURCE: Bank for International Settlements.

derivatives was partly thanks to the hands-off approach by the authorities in the past decade leaving it completely unchecked worldwide—no regulation, no transparency.

Although the 2008 meltdown exposed the derivatives' contribution to the increased riskiness of the financial system, their role since then hasn't diminished much. The OTC market has shrunk by only 11 percent while U.S. banks' holdings of derivatives have grown by 15 percent.[2] Even though there are new regulations in the works, both in Europe and the United States, to bring some order to this market, they won't reduce the risks enough. The chances of the next big financial blowup having ripple effects as wide as the 2008 crisis remain high.

Meanwhile, the largest banks have gotten bigger. Bank of America swallowed the largest mortgage lender and the number-three investment bank at the height of the crisis; JPMorgan Chase acquired the largest savings-and-loan bank and number-five investment bank; Wells Fargo bought a bigger rival, the fourth largest bank at the time. The top five U.S. banks now hold 59 percent of total assets in the banking system, up from 52 percent in 2006. The assets of the world's leading 84 banks tripled between 2000 and 2009, reaching a quarter of all financial assets as smaller lenders, institutional investors, and others saw their share shrink.[3] The chief gamblers have grown in size and can now make bigger bets. The four largest U.S. banks keep expanding their holdings of derivatives; they grew by 41 percent between 2007 and 2010. JPMorgan, Bank of America, and Citigroup—the top three—together carry about one third of the outstanding OTC contracts worldwide (Figure 10.2).[4]

Banks Get Help in Their Derivatives Fight

Regulators worldwide recognized their huge mistake of letting derivatives run amok when they exasperated losses during the 2008 crisis. So both the U.S. Dodd-Frank financial reform legislation passed in 2010 and the European Market Infrastructure Regulation making its way through the European Union in 2011 targeted the OTC market in an effort to rein in some of those exaggerated risks. Some, like Paul

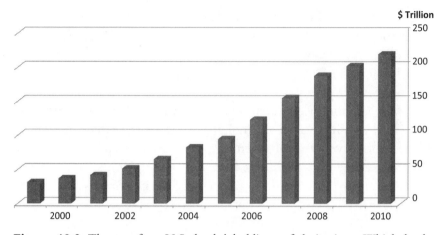

Figure 10.2 The top-four U.S. banks' holdings of derivatives. Which banks made it to the top four has changed over the years. Since 2008, they've been JPMorgan, Citigroup, Goldman Sachs, and Bank of America.
SOURCE: Office of the Comptroller of the Currency.

A. Volcker and Sheila Bair, advocated exchange trading for all derivatives, and Volcker even suggested an outright ban on those exotic ones that cannot be traded on an exchange.

The banks pushed back on the exchanges strongly, since that would increase transparency to an extent that would threaten their outsized profit margins on being the middlemen for complex derivatives. Transparency is the anathema to all that Wall Street does; when transactions it brokers are done in the public domain, it loses its pricing advantage and cannot charge clients on both sides what it pleases. Therefore, Wall Street firms—and all global financial institutions have morphed into investment banks because they make more money through securities and derivatives than lending to consumers and companies in the traditional sense—consistently fight regulation that could erode the opaqueness of any market. And if they lose the battle, then they create a new market that's opaque to replace the one that's rendered transparent. In a way, that's how CDS came into being: As new reporting requirements for the bond market brought more of it into light, CDS became the hidden way of trading the same bonds without reporting them.

Even though the nonfinancial companies that use derivatives for actual economic reasons make up a tiny portion of the market, many have been coaxed to serve as the banks' defenders and become their foot soldiers in the fight against more regulation. That's partly due to the complexity of the instruments and partly because of the end-users' dependence on their banks to get the products they need. This was apparent during a 2010 conference call for the lobbyists of end-user firms as they sought to protect their interests as Dodd-Frank reform bill was making its way through the U.S. Congress. Even though the call was set up by nonfinancial firms, the conversation was dominated by the lobbyists of JPMorgan and Goldman Sachs, one participant recalls. At one point, the JPMorgan lobbyist warned about the dangers of the legislation potentially keeping the definition of transaction platforms for derivatives narrow. Although that specific part of the law related only to dealers' trades with one another and had nothing to do with end-user companies, the nonbank participants on the call didn't catch on to the distinction, and they were convinced by the lobbyist's argument. Time after time, agricultural firms, manufacturers, and others bought the arguments presented by the banks and came to their defense in the legislative debate over derivatives, helping water down the rules. "The banks have seemed to have duped or have co-conspirators in the large nonfinancial corporations on this issue," says Joseph Stiglitz, the Nobel laureate in Economics.

With the help of their allies in corporate America, banks made sure that derivatives trading wasn't forced onto open, transparent exchanges à la stock exchanges. Instead Dodd-Frank and the European derivatives rules demand most trades go through central clearing-houses.[5] The idea behind this concept is to place the centralized clearing company between the buyer and the seller of a contract, thus reducing the risk of nonpayment should one of them go belly-up. Yet that might just be shifting the risk from big banks to clearinghouses, which are owned by their trading members and thus partly the same big banks. If one of its members blows up, the clearinghouse could, too, despite some safety valves included in the rules, according to Craig Pirrong, a University of Houston professor who has studied the proposed mechanisms. The clearinghouses can increase volatility in the derivatives market because they will be demanding more collateral from the buyers or sellers when prices change, Pirrong says. Because such margin calls will be based on the product and not the counterparty's creditworthiness, it could lead to the weakest firm doing more trading as its blowup risk will be borne by the other members.[6] Clearing illiquid derivatives would increase the risks for the clearinghouse, the professor adds. Focusing on standardized trades, which the U.S. and European rules do, is a red herring, according to Pirrong, because there are many illiquid products that are standard. To prevent its collapse during times of market turmoil when illiquidity will hamper its ability to continue functioning, the clearinghouse will also need access to emergency central-bank cash. And if a clearinghouse nears collapse, it would likely be bailed out. "So we're just adding more to the too-big-to-fail list, or just changing the labels," says Pirrong. "Those advocating the clearinghouse as a solution, such as Geithner, were really engaged in false advertising when they argued it would reduce interconnections in the financial system." Treasury Secretary Timothy Geithner has been a strong backer of central clearing.

Meanwhile, the clearinghouses not owned by the banks are cozying up to the biggest lenders since they need the clearing business. The European Commission is investigating whether some clearinghouses have violated competition laws in such efforts.[7] Because they need to compete with each other, the clearinghouses can rush to the bottom in their request for collateral from their trading members, reducing the safety net of their system, says Stanford University professor Darrell Duffie. Regulators now need to also stay on top of clearinghouses while central banks in many countries have to coordinate their liquidity backing for the institutions, Duffie says. "There's some danger that the regulators won't do that," Duffie says, looking at their track record of monitoring the banks' growing risks in the last two decades.

Another part of Dodd-Frank legislation, introduced by former Arkansas Senator Blanche Lincoln, attempts to ring-fence the derivatives trading arms of the banking conglomerates and prevent them from being directly assisted by the Federal Reserve or the Federal Deposit Insurance Corporation during a crisis. Even though this provision was seen as too radical by Geithner and caused him to further back Volcker, it's unlikely to seal off the units that may blow up when derivatives go up in flames during the next crisis. As the 2008 meltdown showed, the banks end up saving units that are supposed to be independent. If markets believe a subsidiary doesn't have the parent company's backing in times of difficulty, then the subsidiary won't be able to do business. "The Lincoln provision won't work," says Pirrong.

Regulators have also pressed the dealer banks to sign netting agreements with their counterparties. If Party A has hundreds of derivatives contracts with Party B, without such a netting agreement, in case of B's bankruptcy, all the money A is owed will be put on line with other creditors and resolved with the rest of the claims. When there's a netting agreement, then the contracts for which A owes B are subtracted from those for which B owes A, and the liability of B is only the difference. This jumps A in front of the creditors' queue and simplifies the debt B owes in hundreds of contracts to one single number. On the other hand, as more netting increases the chances of derivatives counterparties getting paid in times of a melt-down, it reduces the resources available to other creditors of a failed bank. So again, risk isn't eliminated; it's just shifted to different creditors.

Unaligned Interests of Bondholders

In addition to turning the global financial system into one big casino, derivatives have also turned upside down the relationship between a firm and the owners of its debt. When a bondholder buys a CDS to protect himself against a default by the borrower, then he's no longer interested in a debt restructuring to save the company teetering on the edge of bankruptcy. Such a debt exchange would likely mean the bondholder would have to accept a ratio of the face value of his bonds whereas the CDS would pay him the full amount in case of a default. So the $30 trillion CDS market has broken the traditional link between bondholders and borrowers, aligning their interests in opposite ends in some cases. As the EU discusses how to restructure Greece's debt without causing a default, so as not to trigger the CDS payments, some owners of the country's debt may oppose such proposals because they'd rather be made whole by their CDS counterparties than agree to get only 30 percent of what they're owed by Greece or renew the bonds for several more years and face uncertainty of getting paid then.

There are $84 billion of CDS on Greece debt, compared with about
$400 billion of outstanding debt the country has.[8]

Although some of those CDS contracts are owned by speculators,
some are likely owned by true creditors who will oppose efforts to
restructure, says David Nowakowski, director of credit strategy at
Roubini Global Economics. European banks that hold bonds of
Greece and other troubled periphery countries have been buying CDS
to reduce their exposure to those countries. Of course, that doesn't
reduce the overall systemic risk; if Greece or Ireland defaults, the
German bank that bought the CDS might not lose, but the seller of
the CDS contract will end up losing. "Somebody is holding the
baby," quips Alan Dukes, overseeing the wind down of the Anglo
Irish Bank. The same is true with Irish banks and their bondholders.
As the government tries to share some of the pain—albeit too late to
make a real difference—with bondholders by getting the banks to
swap some of their debt with stock or with lower valued bonds, some
creditors are fighting back. There are lawsuits pending in the courts
as well as efforts to get the International Swaps and Derivatives
Association, which mediates in disagreements, to rule that some of the
so-called voluntary debt exchanges were in fact forceful and constitute
a credit event. When the trade association rules in favor of a credit
event, then the CDS is triggered and bondholders (or speculators who
bought CDS to bet on Irish banks' default) will get paid for their
CDS contracts.[9]

Banks used to be in the business of credit intermediation, taking
in deposits or other savings and allocating those as capital to businesses
or consumers so they could invest or spend. Nowadays, bankers boast
of being in the business of risk management. Managing risk has always
been a natural part of credit intermediation because you have to make
sure you don't lend to too many who can't or won't pay back. But
it has taken on a new meaning in twenty-first-century finance, where
risk seems to be lurking from many other sides with the advent of
derivatives, securitization, off-balance-sheet vehicles, and more. There's
one simple rule the banks seem to forget though: Risk doesn't disappear. It can be shifted to others, distributed more widely, but it never
goes away. Bankers consistently concoct new schemes that are supposed to reduce risk. Mortgage-backed securities or collateralized debt

obligations (CDOs) were going to do so by distributing the risk of some homeowners defaulting more widely. It ended up multiplying the risk—by letting banks make more loans than their capital would normally allow, by allowing bets on the housing market without even owning any mortgages—and thus increasing the damage done when the whole thing blew up. "The banks pretend they can transfer risk out of the system, but they can't," says a Congressional staff member who has followed their arguments over the years. Same with derivatives: The banks showcase them as hedging instruments, but, in the best case, they shift the risk to a different player and, in the worst case, just add more risk.

With some types of derivatives, such as interest rate and foreign exchange swaps, the notional amounts overstate the risk because the amount of money one side in the contract can lose is a small percentage of the total. But with CDS, the whole amount of the contract can be paid in case of a default. With equity and commodity derivatives, the losses can even be multiples of the face value. Those contracts require one party to buy the stock or the commodity at a preagreed price and sell it to the other party at another predetermined price. Because prices can fluctuate wildly, losses can be big and surprising. However, even the risks in the derivatives that are seen as tamer, such as foreign currency swaps, can be much larger especially as currencies fluctuate wildly, says Stanford's Duffie. Secretary of the Treasury Geithner, given the leeway by Dodd-Frank reform law, ruled in April to exempt foreign exchange swaps from clearing and other requirements.[10] Although the way such derivatives are settled is different from others, that shouldn't make them exempt from rules, according to Duffie. "They could just be cleared in a different way," he says. Duffie has looked into some of the claims made by the banks on why the foreign currency swaps are safer than other derivatives and found them not to be true.[11] The Stanford professor was surprised by Geithner's ruling because he expected the Treasury Secretary to favor central clearing for all derivatives because he pushed for that during his tenure as the president of the Federal Reserve Bank of New York. Geithner, in fact, deserves credit for having arm-twisted the banks in the mid-2000s to clear backlogs of unsettled derivatives trades and improve documentation, which eased the pain when the crisis hit and regulators and banks scrambled to figure out who was exposed to whom.[12] Yet as Treasury Secretary five years later, he sided with the banks once again when it came to foreign currency swaps.

Too Interconnected to Fail

As the banks convince some like Geithner that there are safer derivatives, most of the complex instruments help to increase leverage in the financial system and connect all the global players into a tightly knit network where pulling on one loose end may bring the whole sweater undone. "Derivatives multiply the risk while distributing it wider," says Thomas M. Hoenig, the outgoing president of the Kansas City Federal Reserve Bank. "It's like an atomic bomb instead of an artillery shell. It's pure gambling, and the casinos are insured because they're too big to fail." The IMF warned in a May 2011 report that the leading banks were bigger and more complex than before the crisis. The largest banks can borrow cheaper than the rest of their peers, and, thanks to the implicit government backing they enjoy, some of the riskiest lending practices common before the 2008 meltdown have reappeared, according to the IMF staff. In the United States and most European countries, the biggest have gotten bigger, and this increases the moral hazard of taking higher risks with the knowledge that they'll be saved. Yet, as we've seen, the problem isn't only restricted to the world's largest financial institutions. Ireland's failing banks were the three biggest in that country, but they weren't too big to fail (TBTF) from the standpoint of either the EU or the global financial system. The same was true for Germany's *landesbanks*. Even Lehman Brothers wasn't that big; it only accounted for less than 4 percent of the U.S. banking assets, but its failure had ripple effects around the world and was one of the final blows to the system bringing it down. There are several factors that contribute to this enlargement of the TBTF tent to include institutions that don't fit the prototype at first glance.

One is exposure to derivatives and off-balance-sheet vehicles that blow up the size of the banks as well as the impact of their collapse on the financial system. German *landesbank* Sachsen LB's off-balance-sheet assets were multiples of its actual balance sheet. Lehman was counterparty to trillions of dollars of OTC derivatives. Some of those are still being fought over in bankruptcy court three years later. "Too big to fail is a short-hand for too difficult to unwind," says economics professor Edward Kane. Another reason governments rescue banks that aren't necessarily the largest in the world is so-called contagion fear. German lender Hypo Real Estate wasn't that big even for its home country, but its failure could trigger panic among investors of covered bonds in the country and perhaps the EU, the politicians worried. If one *landesbank* failed, creditors to all the other *landesbanks* would be alarmed and withdraw their short-term funding from those institutions, leading to their collapse, the thinking went (and still goes, thus they're still kept alive). Anglo Irish Bank didn't deserve to live, but its downfall would have brought down the other two Irish banks because they had cross-lending, similar client bases, and were just too interconnected to each other, Irish leaders felt.

In addition to all these reasons, politicians go for the rescue option on nationalistic grounds too. Citigroup is a big brand name representing the United States in more than 100 countries, and its disappearance would make the country look weak in the eyes of outsiders. The three Irish banks' services in the country could easily be replaced by foreign lenders already operating there, but the country needs to have locally owned banks leading the finance sector. German *landesbanks* may have no function left any more for the financial system, but each German state wants to keep its own.

So the TBTF label may be oversimplistic. It seems to be just part of the problem. The IMF recognized this and used "Too-Important-to-Fail" in its May 2011 report. We could add others: too difficult to unwind, too central to national pride, too interconnected to let go, too dangerous to cause contagion. No matter what the reasons are, the 2008 crisis has revealed that too many banks are in this category and won't be allowed to go down. This has given bank managers even more confidence to take even bigger risks as they "gamble to survive," in Kane's and Stiglitz's words. That can only make the next financial crisis bigger and harder to stop before it causes much further damage than the last one.

Chapter 11

Killing Zombies and Preventing Their Return

I n late 2008, when banks worldwide were bleeding with huge losses from the subprime crisis, and the U.S. Congress had just given authority to the administration to buy some of the bad assets from the banks, Thomas M. Hoenig, the president of the Federal Reserve Bank of Kansas City, called up his colleagues at the Swedish central bank. Because the Swedes' handling of their banking crisis a decade earlier is considered to be among the best reactions and approaches to such a disaster, Hoenig wanted to get some details about how they'd done it. The Swedish officials were very helpful and thorough with their explanation of the way failing banks were swiftly cleaned up and returned to health in the early 1990s, Hoenig recalls. After hearing their story in detail, Hoenig asked his Swedish counterparts: "This makes a lot of sense. Has anyone from the U.S. talked to you about doing that because you have experience?" The response wasn't very assuring: "Absolutely not. Nobody else has called."

The Swedes, like the Americans and the Europeans in 2008, were also faced with two options when their banks fell apart in 1991. They could turn a blind eye to the banks' losses, give them years to slowly

write bad assets down and hope that their earnings over time would
cover those. Or the government could force them to take the losses
up front, recapitalize them, and make the shareholders suffer for the
mistakes that had led to the crisis. Sweden opted for the second
option, unlike Ireland, the United States, or Germany this time
around, and it nationalized one-fifth of the banking system, moved
the soured loans to a bad bank, and turned its economy around in
two years.[1]

The initial U.S. approach smacked of the Swedish experience
when former Treasury Secretary Henry Paulson asked Congress for
funds to buy toxic assets from the banks, under what the administration called the Troubled Asset Relief Program (TARP). However,
the strategy had to be revised quickly when Paulson realized that $700
billion was nowhere enough to buy the toxic stuff. He needed trillions
of dollars to do that. So TARP was instead used to inject capital;
banks were allowed to spread the losses over time so they could slowly
earn their way out, and interest rates kept at near zero percent to help
them do so. Three years later, the weakest banks are still licking their
wounds; more losses are piling up; the housing market is stuck in
limbo; the economic recovery is faltering. Europe's troubles are no
less: Doubts about the periphery's ability to pay their debt are growing,
recession in the weakest countries is into its fourth year, the euro is
in danger of bursting at the seams. At the heart of the problems in
both continents lies the failure to fix the banking problems properly.
But it's not too late. The right policies can still be applied and the
agony of the world economy can be shortened.

It has to start with taking a hatchet to the zombies, to cut the
losses and help the turnaround. But to prevent zombies from returning
(other banks turning into zombies) and causing the next crisis, there
is also a need for tighter banking regulation than what governments
have come up with so far. Just as in dealing with the zombie banks,
the solutions to the problems facing the European Union (EU) and
the United States also require the bitter pill of restructuring debt, be
it the sovereign bonds of periphery countries in Europe or residential
mortgages in America.

Aside from the creditors of Lehman Brothers and the Icelandic
banks, debt holders of the banks were untouchable worldwide during

the 2008 crisis and its aftermath. There's no reason why they should be. If a bank is facing losses that exceed its paid-in capital, then creditors should bear the excess. If the bank has a business model that can still work and franchise value that's worth saving, then the creditor-turned-shareholders can benefit from the eventual recovery and perhaps get most of their money back. When Citigroup was on the verge of collapse in 2008, it had about $350 billion of bonds outstanding. Converting those to stock would have given the bank enough of a cushion to weather losses and made it easier to come clean with all of the toxic stuff up front, says economist Joseph Stiglitz. "That way, you'd never need a bailout of Citi," the Nobel laureate says. "Instead, the government suspended the rules of capitalism and came to its rescue."

Ireland could have done the same with its banks when they ran into trouble. "The best way to capitalize the banks would have been debt-to-equity swaps," says Kevin O'Rourke, a Dublin-based economist. Some of the Irish bank subordinated bonds (those that rank lower on the creditor hierarchy) have since been converted to equity or replaced with lower value debt, but not until after taking over the losses of the banks ran Ireland aground. The new Irish government elected in 2011 is pressing the EU to allow for senior bonds to be included in some debt-to-equity swaps as well, though it's unlikely to succeed because European leaders strongly oppose the concept. Some bondholders of Bank of Ireland have offered to swap their holdings for shares since they probably believe the bank is the best situated among the Irish zombies and can actually be turned around—so the new owners can benefit from the upside.[2]

Politicians and regulators have shied away from burning the banks' bondholders because that could lead to a repricing of bank debt for good, increasing their borrowing costs, says Adriaan van der Knaap, a UBS banker who specializes in bank funding. "Maybe unsecured senior debt of banks needs to be priced higher to reflect the risks inherent in banking," Van der Knaap says. The authorities are worried that such an increase would get transferred by the banks to their customers through higher lending rates, which would hurt growth. That could be the case if nothing else is done to reduce the riskiness of banks. But if the banks aren't allowed to gamble as much and forced to hold bigger capital buffers, then the risk to creditors would be reduced, compensating for the possibility of debt becoming shares. More on those needed measures later.

To remove the shackles on their economies, governments need to end the lives of zombies. If the implicit or explicit state backing is removed, then zombie banks couldn't borrow or raise capital in the marketplace and would be forced to go extinct. Without the unfair competition from weakened but propped up rivals, the healthy banks can thrive, fill the void left by the zombies, and provide the lending needed for economic recovery. "Exit barriers for banks are very high," says Carola Schuler, a banking analyst at Moody's Investors Service, the ratings agency. Those barriers have to come down. Society pays to keep alive banks that should have died long ago.

Who Bears the Cost?

Although Iceland chose not to go the zombie way with its failing banks, the difficulties of winding down international banks became apparent even with the country's financial institutions that were relatively small on a global or regional scale. At their peak in 2008, the largest Icelandic banks' assets added up to one-fifth of Commerzbank's, Germany's second largest bank. Yet the controversy over the government's decision not to guarantee deposits that the Icelandic banks had collected in other countries is an unresolved dispute between Iceland, the United Kingdom, and the Netherlands three years later. The liquidation of Lehman Brothers, which was roughly the size of Commerzbank when it filed for bankruptcy, has revealed even more reasons why the world needs an international bank resolution mechanism. Some 50 bankruptcy proceedings around the world are trying to sort out the assets and liabilities that were scattered among 2,000 legal entities that made up Lehman.

The world's banks have become more and more international; the global giants operate in every country and even midsize ones function in multiple countries. But the regulatory regimes haven't kept up with the banks' globalization. Banking sector supervisors are still national in structure and perspective. Although a supposedly global capital regime exists under the aegis of the Basel Committee on Banking Supervision, the latest round of decision making there showed once again that national interests divide its member countries. The Basel talks in 2010 and 2011 turned into trade negotiations as each member tried to protect its banks' interests.[3] In fact, regardless of where they're based, most of the largest conglomerates are active everywhere and aren't really just one country's problem. When the U.S. government rescued American International Group (AIG) to prevent the collapse of banks that had dumped risk onto the insurance firm, it ended up saving French and German banks as well. Another case in point is the scuttle between U.S. and U.K. governments during the last days of Lehman Brothers. London-based Barclays had emerged as a buyer, but the deal needed a temporary government backing until Barclays share-holders gave their approval for the acquisition. The Americans wanted the British to do it, but the British didn't want to take risks for rescuing a U.S. institution.[4] Consequently, the deal fell through, but it was to the detriment of the global financial system, not just the United States.

The EU, whose banks were encouraged to go across borders and did so, established a continent-wide banking regulator in 2011, but the first impressions of its authority in the region weren't very encouraging. Given the task of carrying out the stress tests of the largest EU banks, the new supervisor came under pressure from national regulators, having to bend the standards to their demands and delay publication of the results in mid-2011 as the infighting went on.[5] "Will the new EU regulator have teeth?" asks Ronán Lyons, an Irish economist. "The European Central Bank has teeth on monetary issues, but when it comes to financial stability, even it has backed off. So it's hard to see how the new supervisor will win the power." Basel committee and the Financial Stability Board, which adds the finance ministers of the Group of 20 (G-20) nations to the mix of regulators and central bankers that Basel already has, have been discussing a cross-border resolution mechanism since 2009. However, the issue has proven the toughest on which to reach common ground, members of both groups say.

The difficulty of finding common ground on that issue comes down to burden sharing: When a cross-border financial firm goes down, is taken over, and wound down, who bears the costs? If the firm is global, can the costs be shared among jurisdictions? Member countries don't want to establish such a burden-sharing scheme. Another hurdle to an international resolution regime is that nobody wants to cede their courts' authority over bankruptcies to a central mechanism or to some other country's courts. Instead we have the Lehman situation: dozens of bankruptcy procedures all haggling over assets that don't have nationalities. The G-20 leaders need to make this a priority. If global trade can have the World Trade Organization, it can also have a supranational banking supervisor and cross-border resolution regime.

The Dodd-Frank reform expanded the Federal Deposit Insurance Corporation's (FDIC) powers to take over bank-holding companies —the parent firms to the deposit-insured banks—in an effort to tackle this problem. Former Treasury Secretary Paulson and others have argued that the government lacked the authority to seize Citigroup or Lehman Brothers even if it wanted to. The new mechanism also requires the largest U.S. bank holding companies to present to regulators blueprints for how they'd be wound down in case of failure. If the regulators aren't satisfied with these plans, they could ask a conglomerate to shed assets and shrink. In theory, this sounds promising, but in practice it's riddled with the influence politics will play on such decisions. Many observers, such as Columbia University's Stiglitz, say the new mechanism will be useless because it wasn't the lack of legal authority that prevented action during the latest crisis; it was lack of willpower on behalf of the regulators and politicians. Even the FDIC's outgoing chairman, who pushed for the expanded powers, acknowledges that regulators are traditionally reluctant to use such authority when necessary. "We have the tools; it'll be important to use them," says Sheila Bair. In a review of the new U.S. regulations, Standard & Poor's rating agency concluded that the authorities may still choose to bail out a too-big-to-fail (TBTF) firm instead of letting it fail.[6] Bair also admits that it would still be tough for the FDIC to wind down an international finance giant and emphasizes the need for establishing a cross-border resolution mechanism.

The Fallacy Over Capital

While an international resolution regime will help deal with failed banks before they turn into zombies, there's also a strong need for better rules to prevent financial institutions from getting to that point. The best deterrent is a strong capital buffer. Today's business of banking is a risky endeavor, so the stakeholders should know and share that risk, instead of unknowing taxpayers who end up with footing the bill when the bets go sour. Debt might have been a cheaper way to fund banks, but it has clearly been wrongly priced, ignoring the risk of blowup. That cost is still being kept down because there's too strong of an implicit backing by governments around the world for too many banks, not even the largest, as we saw in the previous chapter. Forcing the banks, especially the bigger or the more interconnected ones, to have much bigger capital ratios is the only way to shift the risk from the taxpayers' shoulders to the stakeholders of the banks. If a bank takes too much risk and blows up, its shareholders lose the capital they put in. Banks' creditors don't panic and run for the exits. Although a lot of people share these views—including Treasury Secretary Timothy Geithner, who has advocated higher capital standards[7]—there are many nuances when it comes to capital regulation.

Bear Stearns and Lehman Brothers had enough capital according to their regulators the week before they went down. How could that be? Global capital standards were fundamentally overhauled in 2004, basing them on the banks' own calculations of their assets' risks.[8] In other words, banks come up with sophisticated formulas of how risky the loans, bonds, or other components of their balance sheets are, and the capital requirement is calculated based on that. A bank could have $400 billion of assets, but it could hold as little as $10 billion in capital. That capital didn't have to be stocks either; it could be made up of hybrid bonds that were treated as equity for regulatory purposes. That's 40 times leverage: if your assets lose 3 percent of their value, your capital is wiped out. No wonder banks could go under so easily during the latest crisis.

Despite the improvements in the ratios and definitions of capital under Basel III, what has been done is not nearly enough. The capital ratio has been increased to 7 percent for common stock (though some other things can still be counted in the numerator) from 2 percent, and the largest global banks may face another 2.5 percent on top of that. But the safe ratio is more like 20 percent, as Switzerland has done, though the Swiss allow the new hybrid concoctions called contingent capital in the mix. The 20 percent would provide the buffer to the kind of losses that were experienced in the 2008 melt-down, argues Council on Foreign Relations fellow Sebastian Mallaby.[9] Banks scream bloody murder at such suggestions though, arguing that it would increase the cost of capital and hurt lending to the economy. Studies show that a bigger share of equity in the banks' funding mix has negligible impact on lending rates and doesn't restrict credit (Figure 11.1).[10] Equity is more expensive for banks now because they have so little of it and the risk of being wiped out as a shareholder is so great. If that risk went down, equity would be cheaper. Debt has been priced lower than it should be because of implicit government backing for the bigger banks. It would go up if that support is lifted, but also come down if there's enough of an equity buffer to protect bondhold-ers. Bank executives resist equity because their pay packages are tied to stock performance. So dilution of stock—even if it happens once to bring them up to a 20 percent level now—would hurt their pay

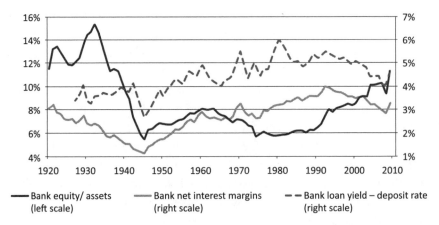

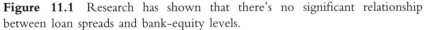

Figure 11.1 Research has shown that there's no significant relationship between loan spreads and bank-equity levels.

SOURCE: Samuel G. Hanson, Anil K. Kashyap, and Jeremy C. Stein, "A Macroprudential Approach to Financial Regulation," *Journal of Economic Perspectives* 25, no. 1 (Winter 2011), 3–28.

for a year or two. However, after the initial adjustment, there's no reason bank stocks shouldn't perform well in the long run. This type of safety doesn't prevent them from making profits.

To avoid the gaming of the risk measurement that capital regulations still depend on, the simple leverage ratio, which ignores risk all together and just looks at the face value of assets, needs to be used more widely and strictly, as FDIC's Bair has argued for half a decade. Max Planck Institute's Martin Hellwig argues that the measurability of risk is an illusion and thus risk-based capital regulation is doomed to fail.[11] "Harsh simple leverage ratio tells you where to look for problems and then you go examine the bank," says Hoenig, who headed the Kansas City Fed's bank supervision unit for a decade before becoming its president. For the leverage ratio to be truly effective, banks' off-balance-sheet assets and derivatives need to be counted in as well. The use of a global leverage ratio has already come under attack in Europe though and might not get implemented.

Inclusion of hybrid securities or other assets, such as mortgage-servicing rights, in the calculation of the most basic capital—as still maintained in Basel rules—will also weaken the effectiveness of the buffer. Bair, Hoenig, and others have voiced doubt on how well the newly formulated contingent capital—where some bonds with pre-agreed triggers convert to stock in times of financial trouble—would work. The United States had a similar product called Trust Preferred Securities used widely by its banks prior to the crisis, but those proved not to provide the security needed.[12] Conversion of the contingent bonds to stock could wreak havoc for the bank, showing its weakness and the weakness of the sector, critics say.

Breaking Up the Big Boys

Even if they're not zombies right now, the biggest global banks are in danger of becoming zombies in the next crisis or the one after that because they're too big to fail and too big to manage. The EU has forced some to break up after the 2008 crisis if they received substantial government support. The U.S. financial reform includes a cap on one bank's share of the nation's total deposits, which could prevent the four biggest from getting even larger. The United Kingdom toyed with the idea of some forceful breakup, but it didn't have the political guts to do it at the end. Switzerland is trying to force the separation of the investment bank arm of UBS, the country's largest lender, and its relocation to the United States. None of these countries have been able to come close to the 1933 U.S. decision that was taken despite strong opposition from the finance industry, which forced the separation of investment and commercial banking. Glass-Steagall's revival (and its adoption in Europe as well) would be one way to divide the TBTF institutions, but it's not the only way. Governments could just place strict size limitations on banks (such as the proposed legislation by U.S. senators Sherrod Brown and Ted Kaufman would do) and force the top banks to split up. To avoid the migration of all the risk to nonregulated financial institutions, such as hedge funds, even harsher size caps should be placed on nonbank players in financial markets so they can never get to the size that's TBTF.

Bankers argue consistently that the big, international, one-stop-shop conglomerates are needed for the global economy. Citigroup officials argued during the crisis that, if they were allowed to fail, U.S. and other western companies couldn't send money around the world and global trade would be disrupted. Academic research shows that the economies of scale for banking max out at about $100 billion of assets.[13] That is less than one-twentieth the size of Citi or any other global player. Moving money around the world for payments, though carried out by banks, is a utility that could be shifted to a global nonprofit organization. Technology has made such transfers simpler and removed the need for any one entity to be physically present in a location to enable the transmission. In underbanked African countries, mobile phones are being used to make money transfers. "It's not the size but the complexity of today's largest banks that render them impossible to manage," says Paul Miller, head of financial services research at FBR Capital Markets. "Citi and Bank of America are so widespread, so complicated, how can any management team do a good job?" If a bank just stuck to the traditional business of collecting deposits and making loans, size wouldn't be an issue, but in today's banking, the model has evolved too much. Miller refuses to cover Citi for his clients because the majority of its operations are outside the U.S., spread out to more than a hundred countries, with way too many different financial, economic, and political factors to consider when evaluating the bank's businesses. "Same goes for the management: how can they know what's happening in all those places?" says Miller.

Miller thinks the largest banks will be forced to break up slowly in the next decade because investors will demand lenders to be more focused and on more solid ground with what they do. The new regulations, from Basel to Dodd-Frank, will also help apply pressure to that effect, according to Miller. The stricter rules could undermine the universal banking model, according to Goldman Sachs analysts. The biggest banks might consider exiting certain businesses, Goldman said in a research note in June 2011.[14] If Miller and the Goldman analysts are right, the necessary breakup of TBTF institutions will happen through a back-door way and in slow motion. Let's hope another crisis doesn't break out before then.

Coming to Terms with Reality

As is the case with most financial crises, the problems of the banks are closely associated with the debt overhang society faces after a decade or two of binging on cheap credit. So the solution once again lies in the realization that we need to restructure those debts before we can shake off the problems and move beyond the latest crisis. Sooner or later, policymakers come to terms with that reality in each financial disaster and the restructuring takes place. But as we've also seen from past experience, delaying the inevitable leads to years of economic stagnation and increased costs in the end.

In the United States, household debt needs to be restructured, particularly the millions of underwater mortgages, where the market value of the home is way below the outstanding loan on the property. While system-wide principal reductions by the banks are necessary, they can be carried out in a way to minimize the moral hazard such restructuring could create among consumers. Many homeowners who can actually afford their payments could opt for so-called strategic default if they saw widespread use of principal forgiveness. To prevent that from happening, there could be several disincentives put in place, argues Amherst Securities' Laurie Goodman. One of those disincentives would be taxing heavily the future appreciation of the home's value or forcing the homeowner to share that increase with the bank forgiving the principal, Goodman suggests.[15] Along with principal reductions, foreclosures need to happen at a faster pace too. Not every homeowner can afford to stay in his home even after his debt is reduced significantly. Those houses need to be foreclosed and put on the market quickly. If prices are to drop further, the faster that happens, the quicker the rebound can start. Since the nation's legal system is overwhelmed with foreclosures and the incomplete paper-work presented by the banks to carry them out, Congress could aid with some fast rules that would overlook the insufficiencies in exchange for serious capital reductions by the banks as well. This is part of what Elizabeth Warren was trying to achieve with her proposed solution to mortgage-servicing problems that was thwarted by the banks, the Fed, and some attorneys general.

In Europe, the overwhelming debt is on the shoulders of several periphery countries. Regardless of the different ways they got there, Greece, Ireland, and Portugal owe too much to be paid back. The restructuring of their debt, if done in an organized fashion and in coordination with fixing Spain's problems, can help the EU avoid the collapse of its monetary union. This would require Germany, France, and other EU countries to face the specter of their weak zombie banks falling apart; they need to handle the crisis the way Sweden did in the 1990s. To avoid falling into the same category as Greece, Ireland, and Portugal, Spain also needs to shutter its zombies, forcing their creditors to bear the costs so that the burden doesn't fall on the Spanish taxpayers when the country's debt is at such a critical level. That will again impact other EU banks who've lent to the Spanish *cajas*. The EU, just like the United States, needs to face reality and stop protecting its weak banks if it wants to salvage its future.

Epilogue

There are several versions of the following cartoon, but this rendition comes closer to the current situation we're currently in. Two building inspectors inspecting a 60-story high-rise building walk too close to the edge of the roof and fall off. As they're going down the side of the building, they look at the floors they're passing and keep telling each other "so far, so good." That's exactly what European and U.S. politicians are doing right now as they push the problems down the line with temporary fixes and feel content with how things are going since they haven't fallen apart completely yet. Unfortunately, one day, they almost always do, judging from the countless examples from history. Three years after Lehman's fall and the onset of the worst global financial crisis since the Great Depression, politicians and regulators keep patting themselves on the back because they've managed to avert total collapse of the system and kept it running. However, the fundamental flaws aren't fixed and the global economy faces the threat of a lost decade with high unemployment, stagnant growth, and jittery financial markets.

In July 2011, the European Union (EU) approved a second loan package for Greece, this time for €109 billion, still refusing to acknowledge that the country cannot pay its debts. Even though German Chancellor Angela Merkel wanted to show her electorate that the private sector contributed to the second Greek rescue, the continent's zombie banks couldn't be forced to take losses on their Greek holdings, so they were convinced to accept a debt exchange to extend the maturities of some Greek debt. But the new Greek patch won't solve any of the problems that brought the region to this point.[1] The deal doesn't reduce Greece's debt load enough for it to afford staying current for long. The banks are putting off the day of reckoning even longer, but they are being allowed to dump some of their risks to the public sector. The European Central Bank (ECB) picks up the slack in funding Greek, Irish, Portuguese, and Spanish banks as their private creditors slowly get paid for the debt coming due. The EU and the International Monetary Fund (IMF) replace most of the sovereign debt as it comes due with their loans. Delaying the inevitable is increasing

Another version of the building inspectors cartoon. Until you hit the bottom,
it can look fine.
SOURCE: www.CartoonStock.com.

the costs to restructure Greece's debt; the haircut from the country's
bonds that will be needed in 2015 is about 50 percent more than
what is needed in 2011 to return the country's finances to a sustainable path, according to Citigroup research.[2] Of course, the more the
banks are allowed to wiggle out of their holdings of Greek debt, the
bigger the burden that will end up on the shoulders of the European
taxpayer.

Meanwhile, Ireland is struggling to escape the same predicament
by exporting its way out of recession. Unlike Greece, Ireland has
several competitive economic advantages, but those have not been

enough to counter the negative impact of its overleveraged households that still need to reduce debt and the zombie banks that won't die. The Irish economy eked out a 0.1 percent growth in the first quarter of 2011. Even though the IMF expects 0.5 percent expansion in 2011, some analysts estimate another 2 percent contraction for the fourth year in a row. Iceland, which did the opposite of Ireland when it came to broken banks, grew 3.4 percent in the first quarter of 2011, which most analysts expect it will maintain for the rest of the year. As Iceland sold its first international bond in the market in June, Ireland remained shut out of capital markets and continued to rely on IMF and EU funding to roll over its debt. In June 2011, Finance Minister Michael Noonan said the country had financing to last two more years, so he's hoping things will be back to normal by that time and Ireland can borrow from markets again.[3] But more of its banks' and sovereign debt is slowly being shifted onto the EU taxpayers, who will, at the end, likely foot the bill as they did with Greece. In July, Moody's credit ratings firm cut Ireland's debt to junk, saying that the country would likely need additional IMF-EU support after 2013 before it can return to markets for funding.[4]

Of course Spain poses a much bigger threat to the future of the union than either Greece or Ireland, and the danger that the PIG trouble becomes a PIGS catastrophe was still very stark in mid-2011. Spain's *cajas* are seeking private capital, some through initial public offerings, some through private equity investments. But the bad assets haven't been completely cleaned up or taken outside the savings banks, and investors are reluctant to take the risk that the country's housing market continues to deteriorate and saddle the banks with further losses. There is also fear that Spain's regional governments could be hiding further fiscal problems, just as Greece did before a new administration took office in 2009. In June, the European Commission warned Spain that it hadn't completed its house cleaning of the *cajas*. The commission also chided the government for basing its near-term budget plans on economic forecasts that were too optimistic. Two *cajas* managed to sell shares in IPOs in July, raising €3.6 billion together. The government seized a third savings bank that collapsed, injecting €2.8 billion into it and saying it would sell the *caja* soon.[5]

The EU completed a new round of stress tests for the 90 largest banks in the region in July, but it failed to regain the credibility it was seeking. Only eight banks failed the tests and were asked to raise €2.5 billion, whereas analysts' estimates of the capital needs ranged from €20 billion to €250 billion. One of the German *landesbanks*, Helaba Landesbank Hessen-Thüringen, withdrew from the tests at the last minute, disputing the calculations of capital levels, casting further doubt on the authority of the new EU banking regulator on the region's lenders. Helaba wasn't even among the worst hit *landesbanks*. The remaining German banks passed the tests, which assumed only a 25 percent loss on Greek sovereign debt while the prices of the country's bonds were already about 50 cents on the dollar.[6]

Keeping Germany's zombie banks on life support has left Chancellor Merkel in a tough spot: She has to look tough on Greece and other irresponsible nations while still protecting the banks who have loaned to those countries, making their irresponsible binges on housing and consumption possible. Thus Merkel played the toughie in the European drama unfolding in the summer of 2011, pretending that she wanted to punish the creditors too, only to be convinced by her French counterpart, Nicolas Sarkozy, to soften her stance so the weak German and French banks could survive longer. Merkel has been losing support domestically, though. Her party and its coalition partners were losing regional elections in 2011. In a June vote on a second Greek rescue, 10 legislators from the ruling coalition defected, a significant blow considering it has only a 20-vote majority in the *Bundestag* (German parliament).

Because they constantly postpone the solution to the zombie banking problem, the Germans and the French risk the collapse of the euro, which has given the two countries enormous political and economic power in the region. The collapse of the common currency would also seriously hit their economies, most likely sliding them back into recession. The PIGS are facing dismal prospects until then. For years to come, they will be stuck with high unemployment, stagnant economies, and a debt burden impossible to carry. The euro's collapse would let them devalue their national currencies, which will reappear, but as Iceland's case showed, devaluation is no panacea. The Irish, especially, are worried that the lack of the common currency could derail the foreign direct investment that has favored their country in the region partly because it has been part of the currency union.

Not only did the second Greek rescue package fail to allay fears over the weakest EU member's chances of default, concern among investors spread to the ability of countries outside the PIGS club to pay their debts, engulfing Italy and even France in August 2011. The fears over France partly culminated from its banks' exposures and vulnerability to the indebted countries. The shares of Société Générale, the second biggest French bank, dropped almost 50 percent over the course of one month.

Default by Greece and other members of the PIGS club will reverberate in financial markets across the globe. It will be felt especially in the United States, where the biggest banks have exposure to those countries through direct lending and through derivatives, especially credit default swaps. The short-term patches to keep the PIGS away from defaulting have saved the U.S. banks so far, just as they did for their European counterparts. Just a 10 basis-point (one-tenth of a percent) move on the value of their derivatives book could wipe out the capital of any of the large U.S. banks, according to R. Christopher Whalen, who rates banks.[7] Concerns over their exposure to Europe helped send shares of U.S. banks down as well in August 2011. Bank of America and Citigroup led the rout, losing about one third of their market value in less than a month.

While Europe teetered on the brink of collapse, the U.S. zombies struggled with mounting losses from the housing market that continued declining. At the end of June 2011, Bank of America reached an agreement with some of the bond investors who'd sued it for the poorly underwritten mortgage-backed securities (MBS). The bank said it would write off about $20 billion for this settlement and other possible losses on its MBS liabilities—the stuff that went off balance sheet during the boom years so the banks could expand lending further, but the risk has come back. Although the deal with the investors could reduce uncertainties over future losses from this legacy issue, it covered about half of its exposure only and hasn't eliminated further risk, Barclays Capital analysts said after the announcement. The agreement also faces legal challenges from some MBS-holders unsatisfied with the paltry sums to be paid by the bank. As part of the agreement with the MBS investors, Bank of America said it would transfer some of the worst loans to subcontractors to service. Former President Bill Clinton said that could lead to principal reductions for the worst underwater mortgages and hopefully provide a model for other banks to follow. The biggest banks, who are the biggest servicers and holders of the largest portfolios of second-lien mortgages, continued to oppose principal reductions.[8] While the losses lurked, the housing market was stuck in a limbo, and the U.S. economy floundered, the bosses of the zombie banks and other Wall Street executives started making millions of dollars again. Citigroup CEO Vikram Pandit was awarded $16.7 million to encourage him to stay at the helm.[9]

Throughout 2011, U.S. banks kept increasing their lobbying activities against the rules that are supposed to reduce some of the risks to the system, trying to weaken Dodd-Frank reform, reverse some aspects of it, and resist international efforts to impose higher capital requirements on the largest banks. JPMorgan Chase CEO Jamie Dimon blamed the new regulations for the slowdown in the U.S. economy. The Financial Accounting Standards Board backed down on another one of its planned changes that the banks opposed. The proposed change would have limited the netting of derivatives on the balance sheet and force the top U.S. banks to show the true size of their balance sheets. It would also force them to hold more capital for those derivatives currently not counted.

Daniel K. Tarullo, a Fed governor appointed by President Obama and one of the loudest critics of Basel II rules that had eased capital requirements for banks in 2004, emerged as a new voice for tough regulation. Tarullo, who wasn't as assertive in Basel talks in 2010 as FDIC Chairman Sheila Bair, is a strong believer of higher capital buffers and less wiggle room for banks to determine how risky their assets are. He could carry on Bair's mantle in international regulatory debates and weigh in at home as well. On the extra capital charge being considered for the top banks, Tarullo was quickly crushed by Treasury Secretary Timothy Geithner, the friend of the bankers. Geithner talked down the need for a big charge and the Basel Committee on Banking Supervision came up with 1 to 2.5 percent in June 2011.[10]

In July 2011, Obama announced an appointment for the Comptroller of the Currency, a crucial regulatory role that was carried out by an acting chief for over a year. Pressure was mounting on Obama to replace the acting Comptroller, John G. Walsh, who repeatedly took the sides of the banks during Dodd-Frank reform's formulation and in the implementation phase. Senators Jeff Merkley, Carl Levin, and Sherrod Brown were among those who renewed calls in June to replace Walsh after he publicly attacked financial reforms as being too tough on the banks. Geithner was accused by some on Capitol Hill of protecting Walsh and dragging his feet on the replacement. Although there were reports of Geithner's potential departure around that time, those were later quashed and banks' best ally remains at the helm.[11]

As Geithner refused to clean up the banking system like his European counterparts, and bank CEOs blamed rules for their shackles, the unresolved fundamental problems of the zombies and the housing market slowed the economic recovery in the United States. After falling for four months, the unemployment rolls started rising again in April 2011 and the rate of participation in the labor market fell to a 30-year low as Americans lost hope in finding jobs. It looked like the economy was on the verge of a second recession in August 2011 as recovery almost ground to a halt, with the first quarter growth figure revised down to 0.4 percent and second quarter to 1 percent. While the Fed's quantitative easing policies provided only temporary boosts to the U.S. economy in 2009 and 2010, it continued to create inflation worldwide. The money sloshing around pushed energy and food prices up, increasing the possibility of further social unrest in poor countries, the World Bank warned in April 2011. Those price increases started causing inflation in the United States even as the economy weakened, raising the specter of stagflation—rising prices during an economic downturn. Even the strongest nation's credit rating came under scrutiny as ratings agencies lowered their outlook on the U.S. rating to negative, based on concerns of rising budget deficits and the lack of plans to reduce them. In August, one of them in fact lowered the country's credit rating from AAA to AA+. That was the first time in history that the United States lost its top-notch creditworthiness.[12]

In the second half of 2011, it looked less and less likely that the politicians on both sides of the Atlantic Ocean could continue kicking the can down the road for too much longer. They need to face the truth soon about the indebted consumers and nations and about the banks that gave them the loans. The cartoon's building inspectors might be approaching the ground level in their aerial survey. The end can be good for neither the inspectors nor the politicians imitating them.

Notes

Chapter 1: Zombies In Our Midst

1. Edward J. Kane, "Dangers of Capital Forbearance: The Case of the FSLIC and 'Zombie' S&L's," *Contemporary Policy Issues* 5, no. 1 (January 1987): 77–83.
2. Edward J. Kane, *The S&L Insurance Mess: How Did It Happen?* (Washington, DC: The Urban Institute Press, 1989).
3. R. Chris Whalen, "Zombie Dance Party: Was the Banking Industry Really Profitable in 2008?" *IRA Bank Monitor* (March 2, 2009).
4. Figures based on Bloomberg LP data and calculations by the author.
5. Nomi Prins and Kristina Ugrin, "Bailout Tally Report," Oct. 2010, www.nomiprins.com/reports/; Jan Hatzius, Zach Pandil, Alec Phillips, Jan Stehn, and Andrew Tilton, "U.S. Daily: Potential Consequences of a Downgrade of the U.S. Sovereign Rating," Goldman Sachs research report, July 28, 2011.
6. Interview with Prins, October 18, 2010.
7. Matthew Leising, "Fed Let Brokers Turn Junk to Cash at Height of Financial Crisis," *Bloomberg News*, April 1, 2011, www.bloomberg.com/news/2011 -03-31/fed-accepted-more-defaulted-debt-than-treasuries-as-rescue-loan -collateral.html.
8. U.S. data from Bloomberg LP; EU data from the European Commission, http://ec.europa.eu/competition/state_aid/studies_reports/phase_out_bank_ guarantees.pdf.
9. Moody's Investor Service reports: "Germany," October 14, 2010, and "U.S. Banking Industry Quarterly Credit Update—4Q10," March 9, 2011.
10. Data from Center for Responsible Politics, www.opensecrets.org.
11. Todd Petzel, "The Invisible Tax—Zero Interest Rates," Offit Capital Advisors LLC commentary, August 2010, www.offitcapital.com/commen taries/2010/august.htm.

Chapter 2: Lessons Not Learned

1. Office of Thrift Supervision, About the OTS: History, www.ots.treas .gov/?p=History.
2. Edward J. Kane, "What Lessons Should Japan Learn from the U.S. Deposit-Insurance Mess?" *Journal of the Japanese and International Economies* 7, no. 4 (December 1993): 329–355; Edward J. Kane,. *The S&L Insurance Mess: How Did It Happen?* (Washington, DC: The Urban Institute Press, 1989).
3. Timothy Curry and Lynn Shibut, "The Cost of the Savings and Loan Crisis: Truth and Consequences," *FDIC Banking Review* 13, no. 2 (December 2000): 26–35.

4. Takeo Hoshi and Anil Kashyap, "The Japanese Banking Crisis: Where Did It Come from and How Will It End?" *NBER Macroeconomics Annual* 14 (1999): 129–212; Akihiro Kanaya and David Woo, *The Japanese Banking Crisis of the 1990s: Sources and Lessons* (Princeton: Princeton University Printing Services, 2001); Richard C. Koo, "Lessons from Japan's Lost Decade: Why America's Experience May Be Worse," *The International Economy,* (Sept. 22, 2008); Daniel K. Tarullo, *Banking on Basel: The Future of the International Financial Regulation* (Washington, DC: Peter G. Peterson Institute for International Economics, 2008).

5. Tim Callen and Martin Mühleisen, "Current Issues Facing the Financial Sector," in *Japan's Lost Decade: Policies for Economic Revival* (Washington, DC: International Monetary Fund, 2003), 17–42; Mitsuhiro Fukao, "Japan's Lost Decade and Its Financial System," in *Japan's Lost Decade: Origins, Consequences and Prospects for Recovery,* ed. Gary R. Saxonhouse and Robert M. Stern (Malden, MA: Blackwell, 2004), 99–118; Hoshi and Kashyap, "The Japanese Banking Crisis."

6. Anthony Randazzo, Michael Flynn, and Adam B. Summers, "Turning Japanese: Japan's Post-Bubble Policies Produced a 'Lost-Decade.' So Why Is President Obama Emulating Them?" *Reason* (July 1, 2009).

7. Rishi Goyal and Ronald McKinnon, "Japan's Negative Risk Premium in Interest Rates: The Liquidity Trap and the Fall in Bank Lending," in Saxonhouse and Stern, *Japan's Lost Decade,* 73–98; Dick K. Nanto, "The Global Financial Crisis: Lessons from Japan's Lost Decade of the 1990s," *Congressional Research Service Reports and Issue Briefs* (May 4, 2009); Yuri N. Sasaki, "Has the Basel Accord Accelerated Evergreening Policy in Japan? A Panel Analysis of Japanese Bank Credit Allocation," working paper, December 2008.

8. Kanaya and Woo, *The Japanese Banking Crisis of the 1990s.*

9. Kentaro Tamura, "Challenges to Japanese Compliance with the Basel Capital Accord: Domestic Politics and International Banking Standards," *Japanese Economy* 33, no. 1 (Spring 2005): 23–49.

10. Charles W. Calomiris and Joseph R. Mason, "How to Restructure Failed Banking Systems: Lessons from the U.S. in the 1930s and Japan in the 1990s." in *Governance, Regulation, and Privatization in the Asia-Pacific Region, NBER East Asia Seminar on Economics, Volume 12,* ed. Takatoshi Ito and Anne Krueger (Chicago: University of Chicago Press, 2004), 375–423; Tim Callen and Jonathan D. Ostry, "Overview," in *Japan's Lost Decade: Policies for Economic Revival,* 1–16; Randazzo, Flynn, and Summers, "Turning Japanese"; Hoshi and Kashyap, "The Japanese Banking Crisis"; Jeff Madura, *International Financial Management* (8th ed.) (Mason, OH: Thomson South-Western, 2006); Winston T. H. Koh, Roberto S. Mariano, Andrey Pavlov, Sock Yong Phang, Augustine H. H. Tan, and Susan M. Wachter, "Bank Lending and Real Estate in Asia: Market Optimism and Asset Bubbles." *Journal of Asian Economics* 15, no. 5 (January 2005): 11-3-1118; Sasaki, "Has the Basel Accord Accelerated Evergreening Policy in Japan?"

11. Takatoshi Ito, "Retrospective on the Bubble Period and its Relationship to Developments in the 1990s," in Saxonhouse & Stern, *Japan's Lost Decade*, 17–34; Nanto, "The Global Financial Crisis"; Calomiris and Mason, "How to Restructure Failed Banking Systems"; Koo, "Lessons from Japan's Lost Decade"; Mitsuhiro Fukao, "Japan's Lost Decade and Its Financial System," in Saxenhouse and Stern, *Japan's Lost Decade,* 99–118; Kanaya and Woo, *The Japanese Banking Crisis.*
12. Statistics Bureau. "Japan Monthly Statistics." June 2011; International Monetary Fund, "World Economic Outlook," April 2011.
13. Patrick Lee, Carlo Tommaselli, and Omar Keenan, "Spanish Banks," Société Générale research report, January 28, 2011.

Chapter 3: Europe's Sovereign Blues

1. Bank for International Settlements, *BIS Quarterly Review,* June 2011.
2. Axel Weber, "Europe's Reforms May Come at a High Price," *Financial Times* (February 22, 2011).
3. International Monetary Fund, "Greece: Staff Report on Request for Stand-By Arrangement," May 2010; International Monetary Fund, "Ireland: Request for an Extended Arrangement—Staff Report," Staff Supplement, Staff Statement, and Press Release on the Executive Board Discussion, December 2010; Landon Thomas, Jr. "Patchwork Pension Plan Adds to Greek Debt Woes," *New York Times,* March 11, 2010.
4. Matthias Inverardi, "German Voters Deal Merkel State Election Setback," *Reuters,* May 9, 2010; "Germany: Angela Merkel's Party Loses Hamburg Election," BBC News, February 21, 2011; David Crosslan, "Election Debacle 'Will Shake CDU, But Won't Topple Merkel,' " *Spiegel Online,* March 28, 2011.
5. Yalman Onaran, "Banks Best Basel as Regulators Dilute or Delay Capital Rules," *Bloomberg News,* December 21, 2010.
6. European Banking Authority, "Overview of the EBA 2011 Banking EU-wide Stress Test," March 18, 2011.
7. Fernando Garea, "Rubalcaba es el candidato preferido," *El Pais,* April 3, 2011; Miles Johnson, "Zapatero Calls Early Spanish Elections," *Financial Times,* July 29, 2011.
8. Gregory Butcher, "Spanish Regional Banks Spark Ticking Bailout Time Bomb," *Property Week,* January 7, 2011.
9. Banco de España press release, "Banco de España Informs 12 Banks They Must Increase Their Capital to Comply with the Royal Decree-Law," March 10, 2011.
10. Fitch Ratings, "Updated Stress Tests on Spanish Institutions' Domestic Loan Book: More Capital Needed," March 10, 2011; Patrick Lee, Carlo Tommaselli, and Omar Keenan, "Spanish Banks: NIM still under pressure and asset quality issues re-emerging," Société Générale research report,

February 15, 2011; David Watts, John Raymond, and Hana Galetova, "Spanish RMBS: Inside Caja Loan Books," Creditsights research report, July 4, 2010; Miles Johnson and Victor Mallet, "Cajas in Talks with Hedge Funds," *Financial Times,* March 25, 2011; Butcher, "Spanish Regional Banks Spark Ticking Bailout Time Bomb"; Jose Alberto Postigo Perez and Johannes Wassenberg, "Moody's Maintains Negative Outlook on Spanish Banks," Moody's Investors Service report, December 13, 2010; Tinsa Consultoría S.A.U., "House Prices in July Follow the Trend Set in Recent Months," press release, August 9, 2011.

11. Patrick Lee, Carlo Tommaselli, and Omar Keenan, "Spanish Banks: Shifting Our Focus from Capital to Earnings—Rising Funding Cost the Next Risk," Société Générale research report, January 28, 2011; Banco de España, Boletín Económico, April 2011; International Monetary Fund, Global Financial Stability Report, April 2011.

12. Carmen M. Reinhart, and Kenneth S. Rogoff, *This Time Is Different: Eight Centuries of Financial Folly* (Princeton, NJ and Oxford, UK: Princeton University Press, 2009).

13. International Monetary Fund, Global Financial Stability Report, April 2011.

14. Bank of England, Financial Stability Report, December 2010.

15. Tyler Cowen, "No Easy Way Out of E.U. Bank Crisis," *The International Herald Tribune,* April 16, 2011.

Chapter 4: Germany's Untouchable Zombies

1. Deutsche Bank, "Building a Retail Powerhouse in Europe's Biggest Economy," investor presentation, September 22, 2010.

2. Finansgruppe Deutscher Sparkassen- und Giroverband, "Winning Through Trust: 2009," Annual financial report, and "The Savings Banks Finance Group: An Overview," March 2011.

3. Bundesverband der Deutschen Volksbanken und Raiffeisenbanken, "Liste aller Genossenschaftsbanken (Stand Ende 2010)" and "Jahresabschluss Finanz-Verbund 2009."

4. Christoph Kaserer, "Staatliche Hilfen für Banken und ihre Kosten—Notwendigkeit und Merkmale einer Ausstiegsstrategie," working paper, July 29, 2010.

5. Leo Kirch accused Deutsche Bank of driving his firm to bankruptcy with public comments in 2002 that cast doubt about his creditworthiness. The lawsuit on the matter was unresolved in mid-2011 when Kirch died at the age of 84.

6. James G. Neuger and Robert McLeod, "Germany Agrees to EU Demand to Scrap Bank Subsidies," *Bloomberg News,* July 17, 2001; Michael Dawson-Kropf and Patrick Rioual, "German Landesbanken: Facing an Uncertain Future," FitchRatings research report, October 26, 2009.

7. Aaron Kirchfeld and Jacqueline Simmons, "The Dublin Connection," *Bloomberg Markets,* December 2008, 101–109.

8. Katharina Barten, Claude Raab, Swen Metzler, Mathias Kuelpmann and Carola Schuler, "Germany," Moody's Investors Service, Banking System Outlook, October 14, 2010. Also Bloomberg LP figures.

9. European Commission, "State Aid: Commission Opens In-depth Investigation into Restructuring of WestLB," EU press release, October 1, 2008.

10. James Wilson, "WestLB to Discuss Sale with Potential Bidders," *Financial Times,* January 15, 2011; Laura Stevens, "WestLB Gets Ready to Cut Operations Back to Core," *Wall Street Journal,* February 17, 2011; European Commission, "State Aid: Commission Extends Investigation into WestLB's Bad Bank and Restructuring," ·EU press release, May 11, 2010; Barten, Raab, Metzler, Kuelpmann, and Schuler, "Germany"; Fitch Ratings, "Resolution of WestLB's RWN Requires Greater Clarity on Ownership and Business Model," Press release, February 21, 2011.

11. WestLB, "WestImmo Sale: Bank Turns Down Current Offers," press release, October 26, 2010.

12. Joaquín Almunia, "Landesbanken and the EU Competition Rules," speech given in Berlin at 9th Handelsblatt annual conference, February 2, 2011; Niklas Magnusson and Oliver Suess, "WestLB Owners Propose Turning German Lender Into Verbundbank," *Bloomberg News,* April 15, 2011.

13. The interview with Kampeter was in March 2011, between the two submissions of WestLB restructuring plans to the EU competition authorities.

14. Bank for International Settlements, *BIS Quarterly Review,* June 2011.

15. Laura Stevens, "EU Defends Stress Tests as Standards Draw Doubts," *Wall Street Journal,* March 10, 2011; Aaron Kirchfeld, and Oliver Suess, "German State Banks Defend Silent Participations in Stress Tests," *Bloomberg News,* March 10, 2011.

16. James Wilson, "Helaba Plans to Adapt Hybrid Capital to Withstand EBA Stress Tests," *Financial Times,* April 21, 2011.

17. Hans-Joachim Dübel, "Germany's Path into the Financial Crisis and Resolution Activities," Center for European Policy Studies presentation, October 12, 2009; Barten, Raab, Metzler, Kuelpmann, and Schuler, "Germany"; Bloomberg LP data.

18. FMS Wertmanagement, "HRE Transfer to FMS Wertmanagement a Success," Federal Agency for Market Stabilization press release, October 3, 2010.

19. European Commission, "State Aid: Commission Approved Recapitalization of Commerzbank," European Union press release, May 7, 2009; Bloomberg LP data.

20. Commerzbank AG, Annual Report 2010.

21. Barten, Raab, Metzler, Kuelpmann and Schuler, "Germany"; Mathias Kuelpmann and Carola Schuler, "Moody's Downgrades German Banks'

Subordinated Debt," Moody's Investors Service press release, February 17, 2011; "Commerz Feels Regulatory Bite as Premium Soars for Tier Two," *Euroweek*, 1195, March 11, 2011.

22. "Vorsprung durch Exports: Which G7 Economy Was the Best Performer of the Past Decade? And Can It Keep It Up?" *The Economist*, February 3, 2011; International Monetary Fund, *World Economic Outlook* database.

Chapter 5: Ireland's Zombies Bring the House Down

1. International Monetary Fund, *World Economic Outlook* database; Patrick Honohan, "The Irish Banking Crisis: Regulatory and Financial Stability Policy 2003–2008," Report to the Minister for Finance by the Governor of the Central Bank, May 31, 2010; Michael I. Cragg, Affidavit presented to the High Court Commercial in Dublin, court doc. number 2010 No. 909 JR.

2. Fintan O'Toole, *Ship of Fools: How Stupidity and Corruption Sank the Celtic Tiger* (London: Faber and Faber, 2009); Shane Ross, *The Bankers: How the Banks Brought Ireland to Its Knees* (Dublin: Penguin Ireland, 2009); Bertie Ahern, speech to the Irish Congress of Trade Unions, July 4, 2007, RTE News video clip.

3. Anglo Irish Bank annual reports; Morgan Kelly, "Whatever Happened to Ireland?" *Vox*, May 17, 2010; Ronán Lyons, "Ireland's Economic Crisis: What Sort of Hole Are We in and How We Get Out?" Working paper, November 30, 2010; Honohan, "The Irish Banking Crisis"; Ross, *The Bankers*.

4. Sean FitzPatrick, public statement, December 18, 2008; Peter Nyberg, "Misjudging Risk: Causes of the Systemic Banking Crisis in Ireland," Report of the Commission of Investigation into the Banking Sector in Ireland, March 2011.

5. Eurostat database; National Treasury Management Agency, "PCAR and Bank Restructuring to Rebuild Confidence in Ireland," slide presentation, April 2011; Nyberg, "Misjudging Risk."

6. Video clip of Barroso-Higgins exchange in European Parliament, January 19, 2011, www.youtube.com/watch?v=uah_BVTmHeM.

7. John Bruton, "The Economic Future of the European Union," Speech at the London School of Economics and Political Science, March 7, 2011; John Bruton, "How Should Responsibility Be Shared for the Banking Crisis?" *America & Europe*, blog post, March 29, 2011, http://intercontinen talnetwork.blogspot.com/2011/03/how-should-responsibility-be-shared-for .html.

8. Klaus Regling and Max Watson, "A Preliminary Report on the Sources of Ireland's Banking Crisis," Government Publications, June 2010; Honohan, "The Irish Banking Crisis"; Nyberg, "Misjudging Risk."

9. Central Bank of Ireland. "The Financial Measures Programme Report," March 2011.
10. "Results of Rights Issue Rump Placement," press release, The Governor and Company of the Bank of Ireland, July 27, 2011.
11. National Asset Management Agency (Designation of Eligible Bank Assets) Regulations 2009, *Statuary Instruments*, S.I. No. 568 of 2009; National Asset Management Agency, "NAMA Publishes Third Quarter Report and Accounts," NAMA press release, March 2, 2011; National Treasury Management Agency, "PCAR and Bank Restructuring to Rebuild Confidence in Ireland."
12. Joseph E. Stiglitz, Affidavit to the High Court Commercial, 2010 No. 909 JR, filed September 7, 2010; Donal Griffin, Jonathan Keehner, and Joe Brennan, "Bono Partner McKillen's Suit May Hold Key for Anglo Irish Loans," *Bloomberg News*, October 3, 2010; "Ireland's NAMA Will Not Acquire McKillen's Loans," *Reuters*, July 15, 2011.
13. Central Bank of Ireland, "The Financial Measures Programme Report"; Eurostat Database; Central Statistics Office Ireland database.
14. Martin Walsh,. "Average House Prices Could Still Be Overvalued by Up to 30%," *Irish Times*, April 25, 2011; Ronán Lyons, "2010 Marks the End of a Single National Property Market," Daft.ie, January 5, 2011.
15. Agustin S. Bénétrix, Barry Eichengreen, and Kevin H. O'Rourke, "How Housing Slumps End," *Vox*, July 21, 2010.

Chapter 6: The Reincarnation of Iceland's Banks

1. Statistics Iceland database; The Financial Supervisory Authority (of Iceland), Annual Report 2009; Magnus Arni Skulason, "Global Housing Markets in the Light of a Global Banking Crisis—Case Study: The Boom and Burst of the Icelandic Housing Market," public Lecture at Lehigh University, October 19, 2010.
2. Páll Hreinsson, Tryggvi Gunnarsson, Sigrídur Benediktsdóttir, "Report of the Special Investigative Commission," Presented to Icelandic parliament, April 12, 2010; Brooke Masters and Daniel Thomas, "Tchenguizes Arrested in Kaupthing Probe," *Financial Times,* March 9, 2011.
3. Iceland Review Online, "Privatization of Banks Draws Heavy Fire," *Daily News from Icelandic Newspapers,* May 31, 2005.
4. Hreinsson, Gunnarsson, and Benediktsdóttir, "Report of the Special Investigative Commission."
5. Statistics Iceland database.
6. Central Statistics Office Ireland database; Statistics Iceland; Government Debt Management Office, Iceland; International Monetary Fund, *World Economic Outlook* database; National Treasury Management Agency, "PCAR

and Bank Restructuring to Rebuild Confidence in Ireland," slide presentation, April 2011.

7. International Monetary Fund, "Statement by the IMF Mission to Iceland," press release No. 11/163, May 5, 2011.

8. Arion banki, "Consolidated Financial Statements for the Year 2010," March 2, 2011; Landsbankinn (NBI hf.) "Consolidated Financial Statements 2010," March 31, 2011; Islandsbanki, "Annual Report 2010," March 29, 2011.

9. "Iceland Rejects Repayment Deal Again," *The Independent,* April 10, 2011; InDefence. "Icesave: We Demand a Reasonable Icesave Agreement to Avoid National Bankruptcy," slide presentation, February 2010.

10. Landsbanki Islands hf, "Financial Information 2010," March 2, 2011.

11. Yalman Onaran, "Banks Get One-Year Reprieve as G-20 Told to Wait for Measures," *Bloomberg News,* November 12, 2010.

12. Iceland Review Online, "Iceland Court: Icesave Deposits Are Priority Claims.," *Daily News from Icelandic Newspapers,* April 28, 2011; Omar R. Valdimarsson, "Iceland May Shelve Eurobonds as President Blocks Depositor Bill," *Bloomberg News,* February 21, 2011; Ministry of Finance (Iceland), "Iceland Issues USD 1 Billion Bond—A Milestone Says Finance Minister," press release, June 9, 2011.

13. Statistics Iceland and Central Statistics Office Ireland databases.

Chapter 7: U.S. Zombies on IV Drip

1. Based on interviews with people who had knowledge of the discussions and those who had seen the memos exchanged.

2. Calculated by the author based on data from the Fed, FDIC, Treasury, and Bloomberg LP.

3. Damian Paletta, "Geithner's Rise Clouds Bair's Prospects," *Wall Street Journal,* November 26, 2008; Robert Schmidt, "Geithner Seeks to Push FDIC's Bair Out After Clashes," *Bloomberg News,* December 4, 2008.

4. Special Inspector General for the Troubled Asset Relief Program. "Extraordinary Financial Assistance Provided to Citigroup, Inc.," report to U.S. Congress, January 13, 2011.

5. Phillip L. Zweig, *Wriston: Walter Wriston, Citibank, and the Rise and Fall of American Financial Supremacy* (New York: Crown Publishers, 1995).

6. Citigroup Inc., "Citi and Wachovia Reach Agreement-in-Principle for Citi to Acquire Wachovia's Banking Operations in an FDIC-Assisted Transaction," press release, September 29, 2008.

7. Bloomberg LP, FDIC, and Fed data.

8. Bloomberg LP data; Special Inspector General for the Troubled Asset Relief Program. "Initial Report to the Congress," February 6, 2009.

9. Kenneth Lewis, "'It Wasn't Up to Me': Excerpts from Ken Lewis's Testimony," *Wall Street Journal,* April 23, 2009.

10. Moody's Investor Service, "U.S. Banking Industry Quarterly Credit Update —4Q10," March 9, 2011.

11. Christopher Payne, "Following the QE Money: Rising Risks, Dwindling Returns," *Bloomberg Government* study, April 5, 2011; Federal Deposit Insurance Corp., "Statistics at a Glance," December 2008, December 2009, December 2010.

12. Sara Lepro, "Two Years Later, Merrill Looking Like One of B of A's Better Moves," *American Banker,* April 29, 2011; Francesco Guerrera, "Citi Plans 500-Plus Hiring Spree in Bid to Close Gap with Rivals," *Financial Times,* April 27, 2011.

13. Yalman Onaran, "Bank Profits From Accounting Rules Masking Looming Loan Losses," *Bloomberg Markets,* July 2009; Jonathan Weil, "Mark-to-Make-Believe Perfumes Rotten Bank Loans: Jonathan Weil," *Bloomberg News,* November 18, 2010; Citigroup Inc., "Citigroup Reports First Quarter 2011 Net Income of $3.0 Billion, Compared to $1.3 Billion in the Fourth Quarter of 2010," company press release, April 18, 2011.

14. Yalman Onaran, Simon Clark, and Joseph Heaven, "Geithner Meeting Barnier on Basel III Creates Capital Pressure," *Bloomberg News,* May 17, 2010; Daniel K. Tarullo, *Banking on Basel: The Future of the International Financial Regulation* (Washington, DC: Peter G. Peterson Institute for International Economics, 2008).

15. Board of Governors of the Federal Reserve System, "Comprehensive Capital Analysis and Review: Objectives and Overview," March 18, 2011; Laura Marcinek, "Federal Reserve Allows Some Banks to Raise Dividends: Table," *Bloomberg News,* March 24, 2011.

16. Citigroup Inc., "Citi to Reorganize into Two Operating Units to Maximize Value of Core Franchise," company press release, Jan. 16, 2009; Citigroup quarterly financial presentations, 2009–2011.

17. *The Economist,* "Taking Out the Trash: The Lingering Toxicity of Banks' Balance-Sheets," March 24, 2011.

18. Justin Baer, "Citigroup Moves Closer to Credit Card U-Turn," *Financial Times,* July 14, 2011.

19. Bank of America Corp., "Bank of America Announces Changes to Resolve Legacy Mortgage Issues and Continue Building the Leading Home Lending Business," company press release, February 4, 2011; Brian Moynihan, "Introduction," presentation to investors by Bank of America CEO, March 8, 2011; Terry Laughlin, "Legacy Asset Servicing," Presentation to investors by Bank of America executive, March 8, 2011; Jason M. Goldberg, Brian Morton, Matthew J. Keating, and Inna Blyakher, "Bank of America Investor Day Review—Just a Matter of Time," equity research report by Barclays Capital analysts, March 9, 2011.

20. Bloomberg LP data as of May 22, 2011.

21. Weiss Ratings,"74% of U.S. Banks Vulnerable to Rising Short-Term Interest Rates," company press release, April 20, 2011.

22. Chris Burritt, "McDonald's Says Bank of America Won't Boost Loans," *Bloomberg News,* September 22, 2008.

23. Greenwich Associates, "Despite Improvements Even the Creditworthy Can't Get Enough Credit," research report, January 2011; Lavonne Kuykendall, "Bulk of Small-Biz Owners to Tap Own Assets to Stay Afloat," *InvestmentNews,* March 28, 2011; William C. Dunkelberg and Holly Wade, "NFIB Small Business Economic Trends," National Federation of Independent Business report, March 2011; William J. Dennis, Jr. "Small Business Credit in a Deep Recession," National Federation of Independent Business report, February 2010.

Chapter 8: The Fight to Rein in the Banks

1. All the anecdotes and behind-the-scenes stories in this chapter are based on interviews with participants, their associates, and others who have knowledge of the events but who wanted to remain unidentified, unless a specific source is mentioned in the text or an endnote.

2. Washington Post-ABC News Poll, March 2009, www.washingtonpost.com/wp-srv/politics/polls/postpoll_033109.html.

3. Credit Card Act of 2009, H.R. 627, 111th Congress of the United States of America, signed into law May 22, 2009.

4. Jeff Merkley and Carl Levin, "Merkley-Levin Amendment to Crack Down on High-Risk Proprietary Trading," joint press release, May 10, 2010.

5. Treasury Department, "Amendment to the Bank Holding Company Act Regarding the Size of Institutions and the Scope of Bank Activities," proposed legislative text, sent to Congress March 3, 2010; Jeff Merkley and Carl Levin (co-sponsors), "Purpose: To Prohibit Certain Forms of Proprietary Trading, and for Other Purposes," proposed Senate amendment, 111th Congress, 2nd session, S.3217.

6. Office of the Attorney General of Connecticut, "Attorney General's Statement on OCC Effort to Undercut States' Ability to Regulate National Banks," State of Connecticut press release, January 8, 2004; Raymond Natter, "Spitzer Cases Affirm OCC's Exclusive Authority," working paper, December 2005; Harvard Law Review Association, "Federal Preemption. State Attorney General Power Southern District of New York Rebuffs Attorney General's Bid to Regulate Nations Banks. Office of the Comptroller of the Currency v. Spitzer, 396 F. Supp. 2d 383 (S.D.N.Y. 2005)" *Harvard Law Review* 120, no. 2: 627–634.

7. Ronald D. Orol, "Sen. Lincoln Unveils Broad Derivatives Regulatory Bill," *MarketWatch,* April 16, 2010.

8. Silla Brush, "Volcker Warns against Controversial Derivatives Provision in Wall St. Reform," *The Hill,* May 7, 2010.

9. State Street Corp. Form 10-K for 2009, filed with the Securities and Exchange Commission on Feb. 22, 2010, note 20 on pp. 142–143.

10. Yalman Onaran, "Volcker Said to Be Disappointed with Final Version of His Rule," *Bloomberg News,* June 30, 2010.

11. Bank for International Settlements, *BIS Quarterly Review*, December 2010.

12. Jim Rutenberg and Raymond Hernandez, "F.D.I.C. Post Seems Unlikely for New York Banking Chief," *New York Times,* February 2, 2006.

13. Basel Committee on Banking Supervision, "Basel III: A Global Regulatory Framework for More Resilient Banks and Banking Systems," published by the Bank for International Settlements, December 2010.

14. Jim Brunsden, "Barnier Says Leverage Ratio May Not Be Made Binding for EU Banks," *Bloomberg News,* May 24, 2011; Brooke Masters, and Nikki Tait, "Basel III Break for Banks in EU as Draft Legislation Offers Loophole," *Financial Times,* May 27, 2011.

15. Sherrod Brown and Ted Kaufman (co-sponsors), "S.3241: Safe, Accountable, Fair, and Efficient Banking Act of 2010," proposed legislation, presented to 111th Congress on April 21, 2010.

16. Simon Nixon, "Will Barclays Turn Its Back on Britain for New York?" *Wall Street Journal,* March 30, 2011; Sharlene Goff and Patrick Jenkins, "HSBC Chairman Calls for 'Systemic' List to Cover More Than 80 Banks," *Financial Times,* March 29, 2011; Phillip Inman, "UBS May Move Investment Bank to UK to Avoid Swiss Capital Regime," *The Guardian,* May 26, 2011; Francesco Guerrera and Sharlene Goff, "UK Bank Proposal Closer to US Rules," *Financial Times,* April 12, 2011; Ben Protess, "Wall Street Lobbies Treasury on Dodd-Frank," *New York Times,* April 5, 2011.

17. Tom Braithwaite, "Greenspan Warns Dodd-Frank Reforms Risk 'Market Distortion,'" *Financial Times,* March 29, 2011.

18. Jeff Merkley and Olympia Snowe, "Merkley, Snowe Introduce Bill to Hold Mortgage Servicers Accountable," joint press release by the senators, May 12, 2011; Phil Mattingly, Robert Schmidt, Justin Blum, "U.S. SEC, Justice Department Probe Goldman Findings After Senate Referral," *Bloomberg News*, May 4, 2011.

19. Federal Deposit Insurance Corporation, "FDIC Board Creates Advisory Committee on Systemic Resolutions," press release, June 3, 2011.

Chapter 9: To Foreclose or Not to Foreclose?

1. Amherst Securities Group LP, "Outlook and Opportunities in the RMBS Market," Analyst report, January 2011.

2. "Top 10 Mortgage Servicers in 2011," *Inside Mortgage Finance*, First Quarter 2011.

3. Congressional Oversight Panel, "December Oversight Report: A Review of Treasury's Foreclosure Prevention Programs." Report presented to Congress on Dec. 14, 2010 under Section 125(b)(1) of Title 1 of the Emergency Economic Stabilization Act of 2008, Pub. L. No. 110-343.

4. Timothy Geithner, video recording of testimony to Congressional Oversight Panel on December 16, 2010, http://cybercemetery.unt.edu/archive/cop/20110401231740/http://cop.senate.gov/hearings/library/hearing-121610-geithner.cfm.

5. International Monetary Fund, "Examining the Ability of U.S. Banks to Absorb Mortgage Principal Reductions," in *Global Financial Stability Report*, April 2011, Chapter 1, Box 1.3.

6. David Streitfeld, "Owners Stop Paying Mortgages, and Stop Fretting," *New York Times*, May 31, 2010; Amherst Securities Group LP, "Amherst Non-Agency Mortgage Market Monitor," analyst report, October 2010.

7. Nelson D. Schwartz and David Streitfeld, "A Plan to Make It Harder for Banks to Foreclose on Homeowners," *New York Times*, March 5, 2011; Alan Zibel, "Four GOP State Attorneys General Object to Loan Assistance in Foreclosure Settlement," *Wall Street Journal*, March 22, 2011; Consumer Financial Protection Bureau presentation to State AGs, March 2011; David McLaughlin and Karen Freifeld, "Mortgage Accord Said to Be Revised as Banks, States Balk," *Bloomberg News*, May 10, 2011; Dan Fitzpatrick, Nick Timiraos, and Ruth Simon, "Banks Offer $5 Billion for Mortgage Claims," *Wall Street Journal*, May 11, 2011.

8. Bloomberg LP data.

9. Ruth Simon, "Banks Rush to Improve Foreclosure Practices," *Wall Street Journal*, April 29, 2011; David McLaughlin, Margaret Cronin Fisk, and Dawn Kopecki, "BofA Targeted as States Step Up Pressure in Foreclosure Probe," *Bloomberg News*, May 26, 2011; Dakin Campbell, "Banks' Foreclosure Costs May Climb After JPMorgan Books Charge," *Bloomberg News*, April 29, 2011.

10. The Congressional Oversight Panel, which was set up by the emergency financial regulation passed by Congress in 2008, closed shop on April 3, 2011 because the original law foresaw its mandate as expiring by then.

11. S&P/Case-Shiller Home Price Indices data; Congressional Oversight Panel, "December Oversight Report"; "The Housing Market: The Darkest Hour," *The Economist*, May 19, 2011.

12. Author's calculations based on quarterly SEC filings by Bank of America, Citigroup, JPMorgan Chase, and Wells Fargo at the end of the first quarter in 2011.

13. Diane Westerback, "Third-Quarter Shadow Inventory Update: The Timelines to Clear the Backlog Continue to Increase," Standard & Poor's Ratings Services report, December 30, 2010; John Burns Real Estate Consulting, U.S. Housing Market Statistics, April 5, 2011; Eric Dash, "As

Lenders Hold Homes in Foreclosure, Sales Are Hurt," *New York Times*, May 22, 2011.

14. Jody Shenn, "BofA Dispute Grows as Bond Group's Holdings Hit $84 Billion," *Bloomberg News*, February 28, 2011; Ilya Ivashkov, Christopher Wolfe, and Thomas Abruzzo, "U.S. Banks' Mortgage Repurchase Risks: GSE Claims Abate as Private-Label Remains a Concern," Fitch Ratings analyst report, February 3, 2011; David Reilly, "Mortgage Deal Leaves Investors Guessing," *Wall Street Journal*, May 31, 2011.

15. Bob Ivry, and Bradley Keoun,. "Citigroup 46% Gain Masks Flawed Mortgages Sold to Freddie Mac," *Bloomberg News,* January 18, 2011.

16. Bank of America Corp., "Bank of America Announces Agreement on Legacy Countrywide Mortgage Repurchase and Servicing Claims," company press release, June 29, 2011; Jody Shenn, "Countrywide Mortgage Investors May Get 9% of Forecasted Losses," *Bloomberg News*, June 30, 2011; Jason M. Goldberg, Brian Morton, Matthew J. Keating, and Inna Blyakher, "CFC Agreement Reduces, Doesn't Eliminate Uncertainties (Now Including Capital)," Barclays Capital research report, June 30, 2011.

17. John Mackerey, Christopher Wolfe, and Dina Maher, "Troubled Debt Restructuring: Challenges for Ratio Analysis," Fitch Ratings report, April 22, 2010.

Chapter 10: Bigger Banks, More Derivatives, Higher Risk

1. Bank for International Settlements, "Regular OTC Derivatives Market Statistics," semi-annual reports, 1999–2010; International Monetary Fund, *World Economic Outlook* database; World Federation of Exchanges, "10 Years in Review (2000–2009)," 2010.

2. Office of the Comptroller of the Currency, "OCC's Quarterly Report on Bank Trading and Derivatives Activities," 2005–2011.

3. Cady North, "Too-Big-to-Fail Banks Get Bigger After Dodd-Frank," *Bloomberg Government* report, March 18, 2011; İnci Ötker-Robe, Aditya Narain, Anna Ilyina, and Jay Surti, "The Too-Important-to-Fail Conundrum: Impossible to Ignore and Difficult to Resolve," International Monetary Fund, Monetary and Capital Markets Department report, May 27, 2011.

4. Office of the Comptroller of the Currency, 2008–2011; Bank for International Settlements, "OTC Derivatives Market Activity in the Second Half of 2010," report published May 2011.

5. U.S. Congress, "Dodd-Frank Wall Street Reform and Consumer Protection Act," H.R. 4173, became Public Law No: 111-203 on July 21, 2010; Andrew Douglas, "European Market Infrastructure Regulation—EMIR," Depository Trust and Clearing Corporation presentation, March 16, 2011.

6. Pirrong's views are based on an interview with him as well as on his May 2011 paper, "The Economics of Central Clearing: Theory and Practice,"

published as part of ISDA Discussion Papers Series by the International Swaps and Derivatives Association.

7. Joshua Chaffin and Hal Weitzman, "How Clearing Helped ICE Reinforce Ties with Banks," *Financial Times,* April 30, 2011.

8. The Depository Trust & Clearing Corporation, "Trade Information Warehouse Data," Top 1000 Reference Entities, for week ending June 6, 2011; Nouriel Roubini and David Nowakowski, "CDS and Debt Restructuring: Does the Existence of Credit Derivatives Make Restructuring Harder?" Roubini Global Economics analysis report, April 21, 2011.

9. Allied Irish Banks Plc, "AIB—Intention to Buyback Outstanding Securities," company press release, May 11, 2011; " 'Credit Event' Ruling Sought for Allied Irish Banks," *Reuters Hedgeworld,* June 10, 2011; Finbarr Flynn and Joe Brennan, "Noonan Says Bank Debt Order Now Effective in 16 of 18 Securities," *Bloomberg News,* June 9, 2011; Jonathan Russell, "Bank of Ireland Faces Legal Challenge Over Refinancing Deal," *The Telegraph,* June 12, 2011.

10. U.S. Department of the Treasury, "Fact Sheet: Notice of Proposed Determination on Foreign Exchange Swaps and Forwards," press release, April 29, 2011.

11. Darrell Duffie, "On the Clearing of Foreign Exchange Derivatives," working paper, May 12, 2011.

12. Yalman Onaran and Michael McKee, "Man in the Middle," *Bloomberg Markets,* April (2009): 33–46.

Chapter 11: Killing Zombies and Preventing Their Return

1. Urban Bäckström, "What Lessons Can be Learned from Recent Financial Crises? The Swedish Experience," Speech given by Swedish central bank governor, August 29, 1997; Anthony M. Santomero and Paul Hoffman, "Problem Bank Resolution: Evaluating the Options," paper presented at the Annual Financial Management Association Meetings, October 15–17, 1998.

2. Jana Randow and Simon Kennedy, "Ireland Opens New Front as ECB Battles to Avert Meltdown," *Bloomberg News,* June 16, 2011; Carmel Crimmins, "Interview—Bondholders Seek Bank of Ireland Rights Issue," *Reuters,* June 10, 2011.

3. Yalman Onaran, "German Push to Delay Basel Capital Rules Meets U.S. Opposition," *Bloomberg News,* September 9, 2010; Yalman Onaran and Simon Clark, "European Banks Poised to Win Reprieve in Basel on Capital Rules," *Bloomberg News,* July 12, 2010; Yalman Onaran, "Banks Best Basel as Regulators Dilute or Delay Capital Rules," *Bloomberg News,* December 21, 2010; Jim Brunsden, "Basel Said to Weigh 3.5 Percentage-Point Fee Based on Bank Size," *Bloomberg News,* June 16, 2011; Brooke Masters and Patrick Jenkins, "Biggest Banks Face New Capital Clampdown," *Financial Times,* June 17, 2011.

4. Yalman Onaran and John Helyar, "Lehman's Last Days" *Bloomberg Markets*, January 2009, 50–62.
5. Karin Matussek and Ben Moshinsky, "Bafin's Sanio Criticizes EU Regulator Over Bank Stress Tests," *Bloomberg News*, June 6, 2011; David Enrich, "Europe's Stress Tests to Be Delayed," *Wall Street Journal*, June 2, 2011.
6. Rodrigo Quintanilla, Matthew Albrecht, Brendan Browne, "The U.S. Government Says Support for Banks Will Be Different 'Next Time'—But Will It?" *Standard & Poor's Ratings Direct*, July 12, 2011.
7. Damian Paletta, "Geithner Pushes for Tough Global Capital Rules," *Wall Street Journal*, September 3, 2009.
8. Basel Committee on Banking Supervision, "International Convergence of Capital Measurement and Capital Standards: A Revised Framework," published by Bank for International Settlements, June 2004; Daniel K. Tarullo, *Banking on Basel: The Future of the International Financial Regulation* (Washington, DC: Peter G. Peterson Institute for International Economics, 2008).
9. Sebastian Mallaby, "The Radicals Are Right to Take on the Banks," *Financial Times*, June 8, 2011.
10. Samuel G. Hanson, Anil K. Kashyap, and Jeremy C. Stein, "A Macroprudential Approach to Financial Regulation." *Journal of Economic Perspectives* 25, no. 1 (Winter 2011): 3–28; Anat R. Admati, Peter M. DeMarzo, Martin F. Hellwig, and Paul C. Pfleiderer, "Fallacies, Irrelevant Facts, and Myths in the Discussion of Capital Regulation: Why Bank Equity Is Not Expensive," Rock Center for Corporate Governance at Stanford University Working Paper No. 86, March 23, 2011.
11. Martin Hellwig, "Capital Regulation after the Crisis: Business as Usual?" CESifo DICE Report 8, no. 2 (2010): 40–46.
12. Yalman Onaran and Jody Shenn, "Banks in 'Downward Spiral' Buying Capital in Discredited CDOs," *Bloomberg News*, June 8, 2010.
13. Ötker-Robe, Narain, Ilyina, and Surti, "The Too-Important-to-Fail Conundrum."
14. Richard Ramsden, Ryan Nash, Christopher M. Neczypor, and Alexander Blostein, "United States: Banks—Finding Relative Winners in a Post SIFI-World," Goldman Sachs & Co. analyst report, June 17, 2011.
15. For more measures to deter strategic defaults, see Laurie Goodman, Roger Ashworth, Brian Landy, and Lidan Yang, "The Case for Principal Reductions," Amherst Securities Group LP research report, March 24, 2011.

Epilogue

1. Luke Baker and Julien Toyer, "Europe Agrees to Sweeping Rescue Plan for Greek Crisis," *Reuters*, July 22, 2011; Rebecca Christie, "Banks Agree to Participate in Greek Bond Exchange, Debt Buyback," *Bloomberg News*, July 22, 2011.

2. Stefan Nedialkov, Ronit Ghose, and Alex Atienza, "Hellenic Banks—Fancy a Haircut?" Citigroup research report, April 20, 2011.

3. Central Statistics Office (Ireland), "Quarterly National Accounts—Quarter 1 2011," published June 23, 2011; Ernst & Young, "Outlook for Ireland," Ernst & Young Eurozone Forecast, Summer Edition, June 2011; Statistics Iceland, "Quarterly National Accounts, 1st Quarter 2011," published June 8, 2011; Gaurav Panchal, "Noonan Says Ireland Has Enough Money to Last Into 2H 2013," *Bloomberg News,* June 7, 2011.

4. Dietmar Hornung and Bart Oosterveld, "Moody's Downgrades Ireland to Ba1; Outlook Remains Negative," Moody's Investors Service press release, July 12, 2011.

5. Economist Intelligence Unit, "Spain: Tough Sell," *EIU Business Europe Select,* June 1, 2011; European Commission, "Council Recommendation on the National Reform Programme 2011 of Spain and Delivering a Council Opinion on the Updated Stability Programme of Spain, 2011–2014," SEC (2011) 817 Final, June 7, 2011; Victor Mallet, " 'Bankrupt' Claim Heightens Spanish Regional Debt Fears," *Financial Times,* June 6, 2011; Charles Penty and Ben Sills, "Bankia Drops in Madrid Trading Debut After Cutting IPO Price," *Bloomberg News,* July 20, 2011; Charles Penty and Ben Sills, "Civica Unchanged in Madrid Debut After $849 Million IPO," *Bloomberg News,* July 21, 2011; Christopher Bjork, "Spain's CAM Will Get EUR2.8B Injection From Bailout Fund," *Dow Jones,* July 14, 2011.

6. David Enrich, and Sara Schaefer Muñoz, "Few Banks Fail EU Exams," *Wall Street Journal,* July 16–17, 2011; James Wilson and Brooke Masters, "German Bank Snubs Stress Tests," *Financial Times,* July 14, 2011; Gavin Finch, "EU Stress Tests Include Writedown in Greek Government Bonds," *Bloomberg News,* July 15, 2011; "Results of the 2011 EU-Wide Stress Test," European Banking Authority press release, July 15, 2011.

7. R. Christopher Whalen, "The World Held Hostage by Credit Default Swaps," *The Institutional Risk Analyst,* June 21, 2011.

8. Bank of America Corp., "Bank of America Announces Agreement on Legacy Countrywide Mortgage Repurchase and Servicing Claims," company press release, June 29, 2011; Jason M. Goldberg, Brian Morton, Matthew, J. Keating, and Inna Blyakher, "CFC Agreement Reduces, Doesn't Eliminate Uncertainties (Now Including Capital)," Barclays Capital research report, June 30, 2011; Hugh Son, "Bill Clinton Says BofA Deal May Lead to Principal Reduction," *Bloomberg News,* June 30, 2011.

9. U.S. Securities and Exchange Commission company filing by Citigroup Inc., Form 8-K, file number 1-9924, filed on May 17, 2011; Citigroup Inc., "Statement by Citi Chairman Richard D. Parsons on Retention Award to CEO Vikram S. Pandit," company press release, May 18, 2011.

10. Michael R. Crittenden, "CEO Tells Fed Chief New Rules Hurt Banks." *Wall Street Journal,* June 8, 2011; Mark Pengelly, "Boon to US leverage

ratios as FASB ditches netting proposals," *Risk,* June 27, 2011; Daniel K. Tarullo, "Regulating Systemically Important Financial Firms," speech given at the Peter G. Peterson Institute for International Economics, Washington, DC, June 3, 2011.

11. Damian Paletta and Carol E. Lee, "Geithner Toys With Leaving," *Wall Street Journal,* July 1, 2011; Tahman Bradley, "Geithner Staying On at Treasury," *ABC News,* August 7, 2011; Binyamin Appelbaum, "Official From F.D.I.C. Picked to Lead Banking Regulator," *New York Times,* July 2, 2011; Alan Zibel and Victoria McGrane, "Senators Call For Obama to Replace OCC's Walsh," *Dow Jones Newswires,* June 22, 2011; Tom Braithwaite, "Warning on Bank Rules Reform," *Financial Times,* June 22, 2011.

12. Bureau of Labor Statistics data; Chris Giles, "World Bank Warns on Threat of Social Unrest," *Financial Times,* April 15, 2011; Peter Morici, "Inflation Moves to Center Stage, Highlights Fed and G20 Impotence," *Daily Commentary,* April 15, 2011; Standard & Poor's Rating Services, "S&P Lowers United States LT Rtg To 'AA+'; Outlook Negative," press release, August 5, 2011; Moody's Investors Service, "Moody's Places U.S. Aaa Government Bond Rating and Related Ratings on Review for Possible Downgrade," press release, July 13, 2011.

About the Author

Yalman Onaran was born in Istanbul, Turkey. He came to the United States for college and realized it was home as well. After finishing the College of Wooster in Ohio and Columbia University's School of Journalism and School of International and Public Affairs, Onaran started working as a reporter. He found himself in war zones first, ducking bullets and shrapnel. The switch to financial journalism was coincidental, but it sucked him in when he realized the powerful leaders of the business world had to be held to account for their actions just as much as the politicians of the world. Onaran has been working for *Bloomberg News* since 1998 in many capacities, including Istanbul bureau chief and magazine writer. He was the finance reporter responsible for the coverage of Lehman Brothers and Bear Stearns when the financial crisis hit. He's currently a senior writer focusing on global and national banking issues and lives in New Jersey.

Index